Herefordshire Past and Present

An Aerial View

Herefordshire Past and Present

An Aerial View

Para-glider over Hay Bluff

Words by **Ruth E. Richardson,**
photos by **Chris Musson**

Logaston Press

LOGASTON PRESS
Little Logaston Woonton Almeley
Herefordshire HR3 6QH

First published by Logaston Press 2004

ISBN 1 904396 20 8

Set in Garamond and Gill Sans by Logaston Press
and printed in Great Britain by The Cromwell Press

*Illustration this page: snow-covered landscape between
Eardisley and Kington*

Front cover illustration: Wapley Hillfort

Rear cover illustration: Hereford Cathedral

Contents

5, 35
Leintwardine
34
66
59
Wigmore
Richard's
Castle 50
75
93
24
70, 72
Lingen
21
Presteigne 22
76
Shobdon
55
Kingsland
15, 81
41
Leominster
92
42
Pembridge
47, 84, 94
89
Kington
45   21, 29, 98
95
4
96
44
68
74 Brockhampton
70
80
Bromyard 61, 79
Weobley
Hope-under-Dinmore
87
82   60
99
68
15
48
Eardisley
63
20, 91
Canon Pyon
Clifford 12
31
4, 54, 56
93
3
6
53
48, 61
Brinsop 96
52
Bredwardine
62
Burghill 49
19
37, 38, 39
25
90 32
Moccas Kenchester 73
83
13
95   7
Ledbury
40   46, 64, 100
HEREFORD
8, 26
97
86
25
28
Vowchurch
67   53
101
Longtown
57
14
Kilpeck
54
71
Hoarwithy
Rowlestone
30   36
69
82   Ross
Garway
88
58
69   16, 19

vi

Illustrated Sites

Acknowledgements

We wish to record our grateful thanks for the support and help provided by many people including Keith Ray and staff at Herefordshire Archaeology, staff at Hereford Record Office, Herefordshire Aero Club, Mr. Andrew Terry, Estates Officer of Herefordshire Council, Dr. John van Laun, Dr. Tony Murgatroyd, and Mr. Geoff. Gwatkin who drew the maps for the booklets of The Herefordshire Field-Name Survey. Mr. Brian Byron has our particular thanks for drawing the topographical and geological maps, the thumbnail sketches and the reconstruction drawing of Wigmore Castle, and other people too numerous to mention.

The photographs are listed on page 102 where a reference code is given. For numbers beginning with 89 to 95 (taken between 1989 and 1995) the copyright lies with the Clwyd-Powys Archaeological Trust, Welshpool, Powys, to whom we are extremely grateful for granting permission to use them in this book. For those starting with the number 96 to 99 and 00 (1996 to 2000) the copyright belongs to the Woolhope Naturalists' Field Club, and for numbers starting 01 to 03 (2001 to 2003) copyright belongs to Herefordshire Council (Herefordshire Archaeology) and we record our thanks to both these bodies for being allowed to use them in the this publication. Photographs which are referenced with a number that ends with an *, or are simply credited CRM, are from the personal collection of Chris Musson. The cropmark diagram on page 2 is reproduced from *Wales from the Air* (C. Musson, 1994) by kind permission of the Royal Commission on the Ancient and Historical Monuments of Wales, Crown Copyright reserved.

In addition the financial support of The Woolhope Naturalists' Field Club is gratefully acknowledged which has allowed for greater use of colour than would otherwise have been possible at the cover price that we all sought to achieve.

Foreword

This book has been an exciting project. It brings together the Herefordshire Field-Name Survey and The Millennium Air Survey of Herefordshire.

As a result of being the first group to win The Graham Webster Laurels in the 1994 British Archaeological Awards, The Herefordshire Field-Name Survey, organised by Ruth E. Richardson, was also awarded a grant by The Robert Kiln Trust. This led to The Millennium Air Survey of Herefordshire, Chris Musson being the air photographer and Bob Jones, to whom we are also extremely grateful, being the pilot. Copies of the resulting aerial photographs can be seen in Herefordshire Record Office, with the field-name booklets, and in the Sites and Monuments Record of Herefordshire Archaeology.

This book uses some of the aerial photographs to illustrate aspects of Herefordshire's history. The theme is the landscape, the control of the landscape and the people. We have been able to use more colour photographs than originally intended through the kindness of The Woolhope Naturalists' Field Club who furnished us with a grant. Andy Johnson of Logaston Press has encouraged us throughout to produce a beautifully presented book.

The authors would like to dedicate this book to our families and to the 118 people who helped in the first initiative — The Herefordshire Field-Name Survey.

Shobdon Aerodrome, near Leominster. 'Home-base' for almost all of the flights
undertaken during The Millennium Air Survey

1 Introduction: Air Photography

One of the most permanent contributions any of us can make to changing the landscape is to dig a hole in the ground. You can never re-fill a hole, or a ditch, exactly as it was before it was dug. Try as you might, the filling will always be of a looser texture, or rammed harder, than the soil around it. Pulling out a hedge, or salvaging stone from the foundations of an old building, has the same affect. This disturbance in the ground gives wonderful opportunities for an aerial photographer because the difference in the colour, texture or content of the soil below the present ground surface can show up as marks and patterns. This reveals structures and sometimes buildings which, from ground level, seem to have completely disappeared.

Air photography works in three ways. When the sun is low in the sky, between October and March, or in the early morning or evening in the middle of the year, anything standing above the ground surface casts a shadow. This throws all types of features — modern buildings, ruined castles, banks, anything — into relief. These *shadow marks* can sometimes be startling, showing plans of earthworks that would be barely discernible by the ground-based observer. Lower vegetation cover in the winter, frost, a light snowfall and floodwater also help to highlight above-ground features.

A change in the colour, texture or dampness of the soil can often show what is hidden beneath the present ground surface. These so-called *soilmarks* are most clearly seen the first time a field is ploughed, or when the depth of ploughing is increased. Regular ploughing drags the soil in the direction of the plough, causing the marks to become fainter as the differently coloured soils progressively mix with one another. The degree of contrast will also depend on the colour and dampness of the soil and possibly the type of feature.

The third phenomenon used by air photographers to uncover the hidden past is that of *cropmarks*.

Most crops — cereals, pulses, some root crops, occasionally oil seed rape — may show cropmarks. Some crops prefer disturbed soil and so will grow above buried ditches. Red poppies grew in the ground churned up by the heavy gun bombardments of the First World War's Western Front; this is why poppies were chosen to be worn for Remembrance Day.

Cropmarks appear due to a series of changes, and stress, in the growth of the crop. These produce characteristic green or yellow marks in the ripening crop, illustrated opposite in the case of a Romano-British settlement at Donnington Hall and on page 2. Both 'negative' and 'positive' cropmarks can persist after the crop has ripened as yellow-on-yellow marks. However, the crucial point is that the crop needs to be under stress due to lack of moisture or nutrients before ripening. In Herefordshire, clear cropmarks in arable may be seen perhaps once every two years. The stunted 'negative' cropmarks and the taller 'positive' cropmarks will also show as shadow sites if flying is carried out early or late in the day. All air photographers watch the weather patterns, the crops' development and plan a series of flights to catch the ripening of different crops at variable times — over several weeks in late June to early August for cereals and pulses, and in late summer / early autumn for root crops.

In grass, cropmarks are known as *parchmarks* and these are of prime importance in Herefordshire where there is still considerable animal farming. Parchmarks are rare, being seen perhaps in one year in ten, when prolonged drought turns the whole countryside brown within a matter of days. This gives the aerial archaeologist a wonderful opportunity to explore parts of the countryside that are under pasture and so normally show nothing. Standing just a few inches above the Roman road through Kenchester is a memorable experience (pages 37-38). In a dry summer the brown parchmark can be so clearly defined that the road's dimensions are measurable. However, grass will recover its greenness quickly after rain, reducing parchmarks within hours and causing them to vanish completely in no more than a day or two.

Aerial archaeology shows sites where there has been ground disturbance, or the accumulation of deposits which may promote soilmarks or cropmarks. It works best in dry summers, and on light soils and permeable geology. It rarely works on heavy soils such as clay.

It is often thought that air photographs will be able to provide us with a complete history of our landscape after just a short time. It would be wonderful if that were true! One flight can show that a field contains evidence of past use but it is continued flying, sometimes for years, that is needed to understand the full extent of remains or to reveal other sites in nearby fields. The aerial archaeologist researches sites, keeps up to date and flies the same areas repeatedly to obtain the fullest information possible.

Air photography has two phases: taking and mapping the photographs, and their interpretation, but only those sites with a very definite shape, or *morphology*, can be interpreted immediately with confidence. Air photographs will not provide dates for sites and only sometimes can the functions be determined. However, Roman forts were evidently built following the army manual and are nearly always a 'playing card' shape. A Deserted Medieval Village has house platforms, ridge-and-furrow in the fields and perhaps the church will be clearly seen.

Most archaeological air photographs are *oblique* views — taken at an angle to the ground surface with a hand-held camera through the open window of a two- or four-seater light aircraft, usually from about 300 metres above the ground. In contrast, *vertical* air photographs are usually taken with specialist cameras fixed to the aircraft so as to point vertically downwards. The photographs in this case are taken automatically at intervals to cover the whole of the landscape and can be directly drawn on maps.

Air photographs are used with a range of other sources, including documentary evidence, geophysical surveying, systematic field walking, surface collection and selective excavation. All field methods use a grid so that the details and exact find locations of artefacts and features can be plotted on plans held in the Sites

and Monuments Record for each county, which are available for consultation. Herefordshire is the first county to place the S.M.R. on the Internet — at www.smr.herefordshire.gov.uk. The 1838–1846 survey resulting from The Tithe Commutation Act of 1836, produced maps for nearly every Herefordshire parish, a few already having enclosure awards. These provide a 'snap-shot' of the landscape in the 19th century and give field-names that can provide clues to earlier land use. Herefordshire field-names are also available on the web site.

Aerial archaeologists aim to compile a jigsaw of pictures. These will eventually combine to provide as much information as possible about the evidence in relief and that hidden beneath the ground surface. Air photographs are a superb, and cost-effective way of finding out about the people who lived in, used, and altered, 'our' landscape in the past.

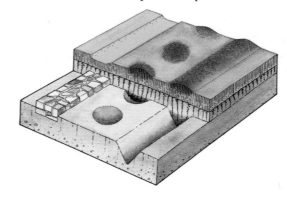

Formation of Cropmarks

When a cereal crop begins to grow, it sprouts first where the plants can use the moisture and nutrients 'trapped' above buried walls and roads. This soil then dries out and the impervious layer beneath prevents access to further moisture. The crop withers above such features and creates 'negative' cropmarks which can be seen from the air as stunted and yellow against the unripe, green, crop. When the rest of the crop in its turn ripens, this colour change fades but does not entirely disappear. Over a ditch, with deeper, looser soil holding more moisture and nutrients, the crop grows more strongly and ripens later so that 'positive' cropmarks will show green after the rest of the crop has turned golden. The sequence can develop over hours in a sandy soil but is more rare in a clay soil where the sequence could take days to develop — and then only in summers of unusually low rainfall.

Shadow-marks at Marden

Late winter sunlight throws into relief ridge-and-furrow ploughing (see page 73) and field boundaries of various dates alongside the now-vanished Medieval village of Marden. In the background is the flooded valley of the River Lugg. These conditions of lighting, studiously sought by the aerial archaeologist, can reveal tiny changes of surface level that are barely perceptible to the ground-based observer, or even to the aerial photographer when the sun is high in the sky or is obscured by cloud. The interpretation of such patterns, once seen from the air, can often be aided by information from other sources, as in this case by the boundaries and field-names recorded on the 1840-42 tithe map of the area. This air photograph also illustrates that what we see is a palimpsest, features lying over each other so that the older land use is only preserved where it has not been destroyed by later use.

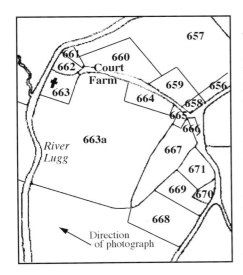

The largest area, in the centre of the picture, was field *663a Bill field*, possibly from a personal name but more likely from 'billers', meaning watercress. The ploughed-over field boundaries, in the centre and left, pre-date the boundaries shown on the tithe and, therefore, are probably Medieval. The picture shows the straight modern fenced field boundaries, one running from the left to the farm with a second running from the corner of the graveyard to meet it at right angles. Both cut across the earlier earthworks.

The field boundaries in the foreground show well. Field *667 / 668 Common Barn Meadow* lost a part for a now vanished school, numbers *669 School meadow* and *671 School Croft*, to the left of the road junction. The platforms left by the buildings' foundations may be seen.

The road turning up, west, towards the Church and farm had been much wider until encroached upon, perhaps by squatters. This was then called *666 In take*, so preserving its history.

Soilmarks at Uphampton Camp

Soilmarks can reveal the presence of sites or features that have virtually vanished through centuries of later ploughing. At this supposedly unfinished hillfort in the parish of Docklow, the scarp slope of the Iron Age rampart stands over 3 metres high in places in the wood. In the plough-levelled field on the right, however, the line of the defensive bank shows only as a band of lighter soil, the remnants of the soil thrown up from an external ditch when the fort was first built. The ditch itself can sometimes be seen later in the year as a dark green cropmark in the late-summer grain-crop or pasture, clearly lying outside the line of the bank. The aerial evidence alone shows that was indeed a finished hillfort, confirming the description in William Camden's *Britannia*, first published in 1585. The field-name is *Camp Field*.

Parchmarks at 'The Moor'

Here, at The Moor, Clifford, the moisture-starved grass in a hot summer has turned almost white above the foundations of the demolished country mansion on the left, and above the gravel paths of a rectangular walled garden on the right.

The Moor was a part of the Clifford Medieval lordship. James Penoyre acquired it in the early 17th century, and it had a small triangular park and a fishpond. In 1827-1829 F.R.B.S. Penoyre rebuilt the old house in the gothic style. The park was enlarged, lodges added and the surrounds of the new house boasted at least three fishponds — including an ornamental one fronting the house, a walled garden, shrubberies and a drive.

However, the impression of a country house is slightly compromised by some of the 1842 field-names. What was presumably once the kitchen garden was now *529 Rickyard*. The shrubberies had become *528 Timber yard* and the road round the estate and gardens may have been to service this. The Moor by this time seems to have been a working enterprise. The house was demolished in 1952.

Cropmarks near Leintwardine

The ditches of this site at Coleswood are revealed, in the upper picture, by the classic dark green marks in a ripening cereal crop (for an explanation of this see p.2). In the upper picture it is possible to see the dark unripe crop as slightly taller and so showing as a shadow site too. The lower picture shows the same site at a later date when the colour differentiation is fading due to the ripening of the crop above the ditches, although they still show as light yellow on the dark yellow of the rest of the field.

The bold double ditches of this large enclosure probably surrounded an Iron Age farm. The size of this can be gauged by using the mature trees, and indeed the tractor, as a rudimentary scale. The entrance gap in the centre of the upper side of the enclosure in both pictures, can be seen by the dark areas indicating the pits of the substantial entrance-posts that stood in line with the banks that were formerly inside the inner ditch. Although the site has been flown in every year since these photographs were taken, it has never appeared again, the field either having been under pasture or the summers too dry to place the crop under stress just at the critical ripening period. If it is too dry for too long there will be no distinct moisture contrast between ditches and the surrounding area.

This site was probably a fortified farmstead of the pre-Roman Iron Age or Romano-British period, of a type that is common along the present Welsh border and is often revealed by air photography. The only way to really decide the period of sites like this is by selective exca-vation.

Snow and Winter Sunlight at Preston Wynne

The advantage of a thin blanket of snow is that, by removing distracting colours, it emphasises the overall 'pattern' of ancient earthworks. This is especially so when earthworks are thrown into relief by the long shadows of low winter sunlight, as here with the isolated church just right of centre in the lower part of the photograph. Left of the church, and stretching up to the farm buildings beyond, are the remaining traces of a Medieval village, in places overlain by the field boundaries and ploughing of more recent times. The whole site is called *Lower Town* and has been identified as *Preston Inferior*, recorded in the poll tax returns of 1377. Preston is recorded in the 1085 Domesday Book but became divided into *Preston Superior* and *Preston Inferior*, perhaps relating *Inferior* with *Lower*. The church was built in 1727 but is probably on a much older site. The earliest section of the part-timbered Court Farm is 14th century and this preserves one of the village houses.

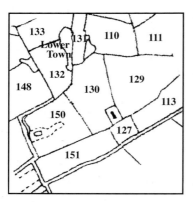

A comparison with the 1839 tithe map shows that the former field boundaries survive. The proliferation of *Orchard* fieldnames (*111, 110, 127, 129, 130, 132, 133, 150*), could suggest a use for land containing stone foundations and, therefore, not easily ploughed. Four of these have never been subjected to modern ploughing, although enlarged by hedge removal. The use of the designation *Chapel* for the fields around the church (sometimes in conjunction with *Orchard*) could indicate that the original Medieval building was a chapel attached to another church.

Pottery sherds and stone scatters have been found over this site and there is a local tradition that the building stone for the present church came from the deep hollow within field *150*. If true, this is likely to be from the undercroft of a Medieval building as the underlying strata is of unsuitably soft marls.

Flooding at Shelwick Green

Flooding presents special opportunities for the aerial archaeologist, highlighting the topography of low-lying land alongside streams and rivers and drawing particular attention to the water-management systems of previous years.

Here, looking south towards Hereford, along the flood plain of the River Lugg at Shelwick Green, the focus of interest is a fine set of water-meadows in the middle distance, flanked beyond and in the foreground by ridge-and-furrow ploughing of the kind described on pages 65 and 73. Water-meadows, by allowing the fields to be flooded in a controlled way in spring and early summer, encouraged the growth of lush pasture grass by raising the temperature of the ground. This allowed cattle in particular, but also sheep, to be ready for market earlier in the year and so to command higher prices, important in a commercially dominated age. These water-meadows could date from the 17th or 18th centuries and may still have been in use in the 19th century. The system was once so common that it was little commented upon and so it is difficult to find confirmatory evidence for particular farms. Indeed, few water-meadows remain as well preserved as this set at Shelwick Green.

Along the left of the picture is the curving bank of the 1960s flood defences, not always successful in holding back water in a valley where travel has always been difficult in the wetter months of the year.

2 The Herefordshire Landscape

Herefordshire, a gentle benign land, bears the marks of all the people who have called it 'home' for thousands of years. They found a landscape formed by huge natural forces where the soil and the underlying rocks dictated where people could best find water and food. It is roughly bowl-shaped with a lowland plain, crossed by rivers and streams, surrounded by hills and mountains. Laid down millions of years ago, the oldest rocks in the area are in the Malvern Hills. These Pre-Cambrian metamorphic rocks include magma that welled up along a great fissure but which cooled before it could erupt on to the surrounding land. The folded and faulted Malvern Hills are very complex but include the hardest rocks in the area. Despite years of weathering they still rise steeply, separating the Hereford Plain from that of the Severn.

During the Cambrian geological period these hills were encircled by the sea. As sea levels changed, the sea floor and beaches formed sandstone, shale (which is compressed clay) and limestone from the shells and bodies of sea creatures. These sedimentary rocks eventually eroded, leaving outcrops of harder rocks to become the hills of today. The most notable of these in the Hereford Plain forms the Woolhope Dome. The top of the dome, which was thrust upwards, has eroded, leaving circles of tilted limestone alternating with shales around a central sandstone core now under Haugh Wood. The Woolhope Dome is special because the limestone, laid down in the Silurian geological period, was a relatively harder coral reef. These different rock sequences, such as permeable limestone and impermeable shales, can slip against each other occasionally causing small earthquakes. Herefordshire is now world famous as the first, and so far the only, area where evidence of the soft parts, as well as the shells, of minute Silurian fauna has been preserved.

At Wigmore, soft easily weathered shales intersperse with other rocks including harder limestone. Again the dome top has gone and the eroded soft core forms the Vale of Wigmore. The harder, buff-coloured, Aymestrey limestone forms the scarp underlying Bringewood Chase. It was easily quarried, although Wigmore Castle shows that even this stone weathers eventually. Quarries are often the best places to see the layers, or strata, of the various successive rocks.

The rest of Herefordshire is predominantly formed of Old Red Sandstone. This term covers red or grey marls (limey clays), fine or coarse sandstone, limestone and cornstones (a harder limestone often rich in fossils). The basically red marl of the lowland plain has weathered to become the rich red soil of Herefordshire. In places this is overlain by hard sandstones, called brownstones, which form the Black Mountains, and by cornstones which form their foothills, the sides of the Golden Valley and hills such as Aconbury, Credenhill, Dinedor, Dinmore and Wormsley. These tend to have flat-plateau tops with steep slopes. If the hard capping has been fractured then coombs — steep round-headed valleys — result.

This is our basic landscape but ice changed and refined it. For about the last 800,000 years most of Europe has been periodically covered or affected by ice. Huge glaciers have advanced and retreated according to changes in temperature. During the most recent advance over Britain the western half of Herefordshire lay under ice and the rest of the area would have been treeless tundra, subject to the icy winds resulting from the enormous expanse of the ice sheets. Glaciers flowed like rivers, gouging out valleys and transporting vast quantities of debris. The last to affect Herefordshire advanced east from the Welsh Mountains, bringing largely grey drift. When the glaciers retreated debris was left behind at the sides as lateral, or in front as terminal, moraines, while the flat valley floors were covered by the drift deposits of finely pounded rock, sand and gravel.

In Herefordshire moraines can still be traced. The Orleton moraine is the northern limit of the great

Wye glacier, its south-eastern extent being marked by the Stretton Sugwas / Kingston / Whitfield moraine. Glacial retreats were not even, with short readvances caused by temperature fluctuations, shown by the Norton Canon / Staunton-on-Wye / Bredwardine moraine. The Lingen valley, west of Aymestrey, where Limebrook Nunnery was later founded, is typical of the flat-bottomed, steep sided valleys left by a retreating glacier, as is part of the Golden Valley. However, the River Teme was the most affected locally by these huge forces. It emptied into the River Lugg until ice blocked its path, changing its course to join the River Severn near Worcester.

Such vast topographical changes were compounded by melting ice as the climate became warmer and the sheer size of some valleys shows the force of the currents that swept through them. Depressions, between surrounding harder rock, turned into lakes, as around Letton where the moraine acted as a dam. A similar lake appeared at Dorstone and the area can still be marshy. Part of Wigmore, in the flat lower valley, is still poorly drained, which helped to create the late Medieval landscape.

All these changes led to the formation of soils that would later make Herefordshire so productive. The consistency and soil quality varies according to the type and hardness of the underlying rock. The Malvern Hills have a higher rainfall but the water drains off quickly leaving the highest parts very dry.

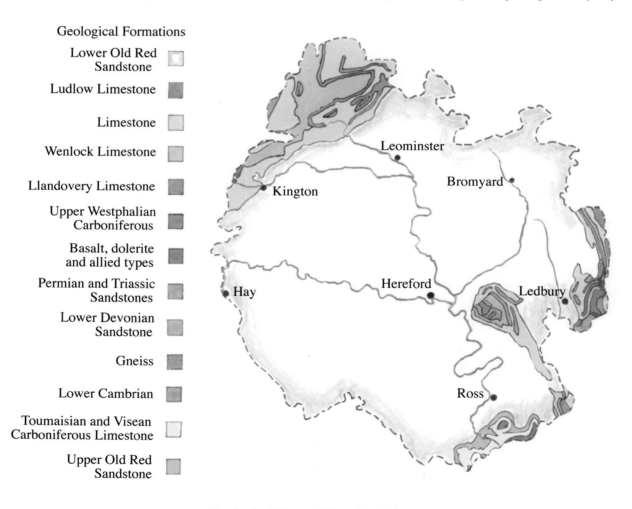

Geological Formations

Lower Old Red Sandstone

Ludlow Limestone

Limestone

Wenlock Limestone

Llandovery Limestone

Upper Westphalian Carboniferous

Basalt, dolerite and allied types

Permian and Triassic Sandstones

Lower Devonian Sandstone

Gneiss

Lower Cambrian

Toumaisian and Visean Carboniferous Limestone

Upper Old Red Sandstone

Geological Map of Herefordshire

Indeed the name Malvern comes from the Welsh *moel bryn*, meaning bare hill, and certainly the ridge has never been tree-covered. Indeed, the grass here is of a very distinctive species.

However, the Herefordshire lowlands, 65% of the area, are different. They are overlain by glacial drift and divided into the central area of red marls giving a heavy close-textured loam soil, the south-eastern area of sandstones giving a lighter, sandy soil, and the riverlands of the Wye, Lugg, Frome and Arrow. Most of the area is within the rain-shadow of the Black Mountains so there is enough rain but not too much.

During the warmer Mesolithic, from *c.*8000 B.C., the land became clothed with vegetation. In time woods gradually took over the bare post-glacial land-scape, in time changing from pine and birch to broadleaved deciduous trees like oak. Their roots helped to hold the soil, put nutrients into it, and made it extremely fertile. Ancient woodland, as in parts of Haugh Wood, is often marked by lime trees.

Today, the best soil supports a variety of crops, giving consistently high yields. The northern deep mudstones grow fruit. Hops are possible but cannot survive in standing water. Drainage is all-important, benefiting crops by raising the summer soil temperature. The southern lighter sandy soils are easier to work, supporting a range of arable crops. Different soils grow different wild plants, beech trees thriving on limestone. Wild flowers include snowdrops, cowslips, bluebells and wood anemone.

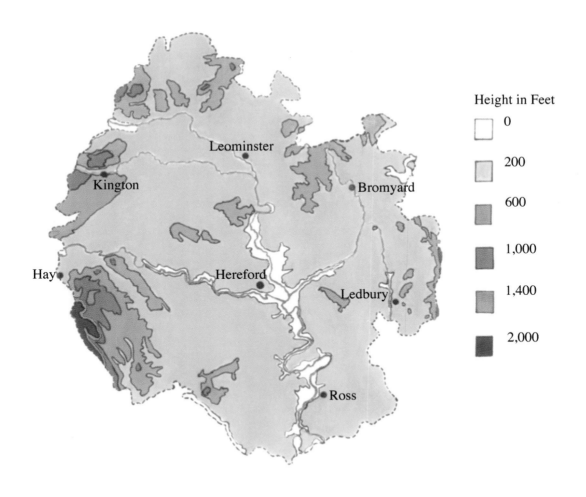

Topographical Map of Herefordshire

Lugg Valley under snow

This spectacular photograph of the meandering River Lugg, looking south towards Shelwick, shows sinuous flood-banks on either side. The shape and relief are emphasised by the low light and the light snowfall which virtually eliminates distracting colour. Several field boundaries, which met the river in 1844, now end at the flood-banks. The minor road crosses the river at Wergins Bridge, bottom right. To the left of the river, centre, a field boundary, with trees on it, preserves the line of the Hereford–Gloucester Canal, completed in 1845. The modern railway line from the north to Hereford, top right, is the curve just above centre, extreme right.

The Wye Valley, looking west from Old Castleton

Beyond the river meadows and meanders of the River Wye flood plain there rise the snow-clad Welsh hills. In the foreground, on a hillock overlooking a steep fall down to the flood plain, is the motte-and-bailey castle of Old Castleton, once held by Ralph de Todini. It was probably one of the many built by William fitzOsbern of Breteuil, created Earl of Hereford in 1067 by William the Conqueror.

Longtown to Black Hill

The distinctive north-south ridges of this part of Herefordshire show the linear village of Longtown on the lower ridge to the right, in the rain shadow of the Black Mountains. The Black Hill, top centre, immortalised by Bruce Chatwin in *On the Black Hill*, is known locally as the Cat's Back from its shape. Left of the Longtown ridge is the Olchon Valley. In the foreground, above the farm at bottom left is the Medieval motte-and-bailey castle of Pont-hendre (see page 54).

Herefordshire landscapes at Dinmore Hill (top) and Eywood (bottom)

The fertile landscape of central Herefordshire is seen looking south across Dinmore Hill, towards Hereford. The A49 road strikes over the hill, while the railway uses tunnels through it.

Eywood, formerly the seat of the Harley family, Earls of Oxford and Mortimer, stood, before demolition in 1958, just left of centre. In the foreground is Flintsham Pool, which being on low ground, may have been naturally formed after the Ice Age in this area of moraine and drumlins, being one of a series running north-east towards Staunton-on-Arrow and Shobdon. Above it is Garden Wood, part of the 18th-century landscaping. Titley Pool, beyond and right, was deliberately formed by flooding *Fowle Meadow*, which sounds as if the land flooded anyway! Over 100 bird species have been recorded here.

3 Early Man

The Palaeolithic (Old Stone Age)

The incredibly rich site of King Arthur's Cave on the Doward, with possibly the longest occupation sequence, though not continuous, in Britain, is located on the side of a dry valley leading down to the River Wye, which has since formed its spectacular gorge. The earliest dated remains in the cave are two mammoth teeth radiocarbon dated to 34-38,000 years ago — the Palaeolithic, or Old Stone Age. Later visitors were cave lion, woolly rhinoceros, and hyena. The earliest date for people is 12,000 years ago from a red deer bone showing butchery marks — it had been smashed to obtain the protein-rich marrow. At this level there are long flint blades and the animals hunted included giant deer, horse, bison and reindeer. Hunters temporarily camped in the mouth of the cave, not inside it, and it seems used the dry valley to corner these large and dangerous animals. They also left two sea-shells. Caves and rock shelters were used by animals and occasionally by people.

The Mesolithic (Middle Stone Age)

It is the Mesolithic people who start to have home bases, though none has yet been found in Herefordshire. Apart from the Doward, evidence is known from the Golden Valley and around Ledbury. By cutting down trees to create glades open to the sun people allowed new succulent shoots to grow attracting grazing animals, and so making it easier for hunters to find them when meat was wanted. Life was a Garden of Eden compared with previous periods. There was plenty to eat in the fruits, vegetables, nuts, birds, animals and, as time went on, an increasing variety of fish. There was every incentive to settle and, anyway, change was coming. By 6000 B.C. the great lake of the North Sea, swollen by the melt water from the retreating ice, had broken through, breaking the rock plug towering above the plain between Britain and the Continent, forming what is now the English Channel. This must have been sudden and catastrophic for anyone caught in its path. Mesolithic camp sites were drowned and people and animals in Britain could no longer migrate if food became scarce. Now the only way in, or out, of Britain was by sea.

The Neolithic (New Stone Age)

The Neolithic is marked by the start of farming, not just harvesting but the deliberate sowing and care of crops and the continuous care of penned animals. Domesticated cereals were developed from wild plants which grew in the Near East. Einkorn wheat is known from as early as 7000 B.C. as is emmer wheat, which crossed with a wild grass became the corn of the great civilisations of Mesopotamia and Egypt. Barley, which can grow in less favourable conditions, was also domesticated at about the same time. None of these cereals grew wild in Europe and when farming is first found in Britain, from c.4000 B.C., it is the domesticated strains that are present. So seed corn was imported. It is probable that domesticated cattle, pigs, sheep and goats were also imported. Log dug-outs would not have been large enough to transport such animals and so rafts, or possibly skin-covered boats, must have been used. It is likely that the people bringing this seed corn and stock came from Brittany and the Lower Rhine valley. There need only have been a few of them because successful farms, providing sufficient food to augment hunting and gathering, could have been copied. It took a thousand years for farming to spread all over Britain.

Finding such farms can be a problem for the archaeologist, whether ground-based or in the air, as houses were made from local resources. In Herefordshire this was largely timber, which rarely survives unless burnt or has remained in water-logged conditions. At Dorstone, a settlement estimated to have been of perhaps thirty families, was enclosed by a stone wall with possibly a fence on top. The enclo-

Wye Gorge at Little Doward (opposite)

sure contained hut floors, storage pits, pottery, and worked flint, including polished stone axes, brought from Wales and the Cotswolds.

Finds from other parts of the country include Penzance greenstone at Elton and St. Margarets, and axes originally from Cumbria and Gwynedd at Almeley and Weobley. The valleys of the River Arrow and Teme have also produced Neolithic finds, showing that trees were being felled. Neolithic people could manage woodland and the Somerset Levels show evidence for coppicing and skilled woodcraft. As farmers, they understood the quality of the soil by observing the vegetation. Limewoods would have been cleared for fields, as limes grow on very fertile soil, and wood ash could have been used as a fertiliser. Once the best soil was utilised people had to clear plots on hillsides and in less favourable areas often covered with stones. The stones would have been removed to lower down the slope and used to prevent the soil from slipping downhill during regular tillage. Such fields gradually became terraces held by 'lynchets', stone embankments concealed under earth and vegetation. Although lynchets can date from any subsequent period, a few may be Neolithic. Small fields can be worked by hand with spade and hoe but these farmers also had an ard, a light, wooden plough with a stone point. It did not turn the soil — it simply made a furrow for the seed through the fertile topsoil.

However, farming brought difficulties. People had to protect crops and livestock and they could not readily move if crops failed or livestock died of disease. Experience and trial-and-error led to the eventual introduction of rotation and manuring, probably in the Bronze Age, which would have helped maintain yields. Meanwhile, however, people came to rely on a very few crops, giving them a less varied and less nutritional diet than their hunter-gatherer predecessors. Grinding corn on a quern was back-breaking repetitive work that could lead to damage of the vertebrae and joints, causing arthritis. Life could be very short. Pigs, rooting in woods and grubbing up invasive bracken, increased in number. They were the popular meat for the feasts, some of which were a part of burial ceremonies and ritual gatherings.

Neolithic long barrows were stone chambers used for burials, covered with an elongated mound of earth and often orientated towards the mid-winter solstice. They housed the bones of several people, even up to more than fifty, all apparently buried as equals in the stone-built chambers often at one end within the mound of the tomb. There is no indication of one person being more important than another. Near the Dorstone settlement are two long barrows — Arthur's Stone and Lodge Farm Long Barrow. Pillaged long ago, Arthur's Stone still provides evidence for the religion of the time. It is placed on the ridge of Merbach Hill and, overlooking the farmland of the people, suggests a territorial marker laying claim to it. Perhaps they thought their ancestors protected them as they worked, giving them a right to this land.

From Neolithic to The Bronze Age

So far, there is no trace in Herefordshire of the earliest communal monuments, known as causewayed enclosures from the number of entrances through their enclosing banks and ditches. The first phase of Stonehenge belongs to this period and indeed it may have originally been a causewayed enclosure. Such enclosures went out of use in the later Neolithic and henges, the most famous example of which is Avebury in Wiltshire, began to be constructed. Many henges had a pronounced bank with an interior ditch, isolating the ritual area in the centre. Some had only one entrance, but others, dated perhaps to c.2500 - 2000 B.C., had more than one. Henges are being tentatively recognised in Herefordshire, often only as cropmarks, at Adforton, Clifford, Eardisley, Madley and Whitney, but none has as yet been excavated or confirmed as such. In addition, the end of a cursus, that most enigmatic of Neolithic monuments and a part of the Radnor ritual landscape, runs into Herefordshire.

Finding the sites of Bronze Age farms is extremely difficult. Even fields are hard to trace, though boundaries may be identified by a pattern of very long strips suggesting someone in overall control. That there was an elite, whether secular or religious, is indicated by the change in burials. Bronze Age round barrows came into use, housing

Palaeolithic and Mesolithic rock-shelters in the Wye Gorge
In early times caves and rock-shelters provided seasonal protection for the nomadic hunter-gatherers of the day. The Madawg rock-shelter, seen here at lower right, produced a necklace of ten pierced cowrie shells and a periwinkle from a Late Mesolithic layer. Someone brought these shells from the coast, probably in late summer to judge by the charred hawthorn and other environmental evidence with which they were associated. This shows how mobile people were even then. They had flint-tipped wooden spears and arrows, or used small microliths fitted into bone or wooden handles with beeswax and resin to make a serrated edge. Other evidence of Mesolithic occupation has been found in Colwall, Kington, Sarnesfield and Tupsley.

single primary burials. However, there are not enough barrows to account for everyone. The boy buried with his knife and beaker in such a barrow in an Aymestrey quarry was too young to have achieved a status himself, and so shows that family connections were important. This was a cist burial similar to those found in the Olchon Valley, Longtown. Later burials dispensed with the stone cist but still raised a mound of earth and stones, often with a surrounding ditch, over the primary internment. Sometimes secondary burials, perhaps of family members, were inserted into existing round barrows. These burials were often grouped together into cemeteries. The Herefordshire area has several such cemeteries as well as apparently isolated round barrows, each probably near to the farms and land that belonged to the barrow occupants. Interestingly, many are found near rivers, perhaps suggesting water was important in the ritual of these farming communities. The arrangement of the stones now erected at Stonehenge reinforced the importance of the midwinter solstice, when ceremonies would be held to plead for a return of the light and warmth of spring — crucial for crop-growing. Even today people celebrate in mid-winter. What is certain is that some sort of 'class system' had arrived — most Bronze Age people's burials were not permanently recorded in the landscape.

Arthur's Stone Long Barrow
The mound originally covered the whole tomb, extending at least to the hedge on the right and across the road at lower left. The tomb is considered to be similar to long barrows in the Severn-Cotswold area. The huge capstone of the central burial chamber can be seen, centre. The original entrance passage was to the left of the capstone. The single stone, right, probably served as a false door when the tomb was in use. If so, then this would have been the focal point for ceremonies when each new internment was made.

The Camp, a possible henge near Eardisley
This earthwork enclosure shows prominently as a shadow site under snow, the banks appearing to be *outside* rather than *inside* the ditch. Following this aerial photograph, a geophysical survey was carried out which demonstrated that the site is precisely circular with two opposing entrances. A henge was suggested, though the possibility remains as yet unconfirmed, and an alternative is that it is a Medieval ringwork. The parish boundary is marked by the hedge running diagonally from top left to bottom right, bending around the monument and indicating that the earthwork was prominent in the landscape when the earlier parish boundary was finally fixed in the 12th to 13th centuries.

Bronze Age Barrow at Byton

This is one of Herefordshire's Bronze Age round barrows, centre right, that still survives as an earthwork on low land, amid the present fields, here under snow. Another barrow nearby, not in this picture, has been virtually levelled by ploughing.

Bronze Age round barrows are found in different shapes. The most common, used by both men and women, was a bowl-barrow, a mound within a circular ditch and sometimes an outer bank. Variations are bell-barrows which seem to have been for males, disc-barrows for females, saucer-barrows and pond-barrows. The size was no indication of the wealth of the burial. Most of the ones found in Herefordshire appear to be bowl-barrows but erosion could mask details.

This photograph also shows ridge-and-furrow in the foreground.

Ring-ditches at Pembridge

Three round barrows, one of them oval shaped, show here as cropmark ring-ditches, which with further barrows nearby, constitute a cemetery. This close-up view shows one of the barrows very clearly in the centre of the photograph with another, less clearly marked, some distance to the left. The oval shape of the small ring-ditch to the right is unusual but known from a number of sites in southern Britain. The mounds heaped up from these ditches have long been flattened by ploughing, leaving the ring-ditches, as the only sign of their former existence. The dark area, centre, represents deeper soil in the wide meander of a former streambed.

4 The Iron Age

In the Iron Age, from *c.*600 B.C., for the first time settlements can be found over the whole of Herefordshire. Indeed, it is likely that farms were numerous but most of these are difficult to trace now and many may lie under modern farms that are still cultivating the same fields as in the Iron Age. In fact it is easier to find Iron Age hillforts which were the dominant Iron Age sites being located to give views over wide areas of countryside. There are at least 53 in and around the county with more medium-sized ones than elsewhere in Britain. These are well-defended, normally having only one entrance, and two-thirds are multivallate. In contrast, the majority of the large hillforts have two entrances, are univallate — that is with a single, often massive, bank and ditch — and several overlook the areas with the most fertile and productive soils. Of the five large multi-vallate hillforts in, and around, the area, only Burfa, just in Radnorshire, has a single enclosure, while Herefordshire Beacon, Little Doward, Croft Ambrey and Ivington have two or more, suggesting that their multiple enclosures could have been used for different purposes, possibly stock rearing. While Titterstone Clee, in southern Shropshire, towering above Ludlow, is the largest hillfort in the area, Credenhill, at 50 acres and overlooking superb soil, is so central to the Herefordshire plain as to suggest a tribal capital.

Many hillforts may have originated as Bronze Age villages, with palisades or banks large enough to deter wild animals but not a determined attack. They can be enormous, and the organisation of the manpower, food and water resources needed for their construction and maintenance points to some kind of central control. The banks, heightened by steeply dug ditches, even as at Capler cut into the bedrock, may have been topped by a stout wooden fence or palisade made by felling local trees, perhaps oak, ash, hazel, or field maple. Hillforts were often altered, enlarged or reduced in size. Entrances, the weak points, were rebuilt many times over, sometimes with 'guard chambers', as at Croft Ambrey and Midsummer Hill.

Difficulties caused by the rise in population were compounded by climatic changes in the late Bronze Age, made worse by Mount Hekla's massive volcanic eruption in Iceland in 1150 B.C. Uncertain times led to religious changes, focusing far more on water gods, with offerings thrown into rivers, lakes and bogs. In the cooler, wetter climate, from about 1000 B.C., marginal land could no longer be farmed. Changes came quickly. Crops would rot and animals became diseased. A family might try to cope by eating seed-corn and killing livestock but by the second year the options were to move or starve — but moving meant encroaching on land already settled. People would defend their own land and conflict resulted — and this, perhaps, provided the back-ground to hillfort construction. Fighting was short and sharp as hillforts were not meant to withstand sieges. Few had internal water supplies — in and around Herefordshire, only Credenhill, Midsummer Hill and Titterstone Clee had springs. Cattle, needing water and pasture, could only be brought temporarily within the defences, and cattle were important as they probably were then a sign of wealth.

Ploughing used a bow-ard, usually of oak and with iron replacing the stone share tip of earlier times. Grain grown was mainly rye, two types of barley, and four types of wheat, including emmer and spelt, both of which were picked by hand, the stalks being cut later. This early wheat contained about twice the protein of modern bread-wheat. 'Weeds' that grew amongst the corn were also often used, notably fat hen, useful as a vegetable, for fodder and possibly for flour. Other crops included oats, peas, beans, flax for fibre and oil, and poppies. Farming in the Herefordshire area is shown by carbonised grain in pits and postholes, querns, sickles and four-post

Wapley Hillfort (opposite)

buildings interpreted as granaries, notably within the great hillfort at Croft Ambrey.

The cooler climate led to increased rainfall and over time this improved the grasses and so cereals. Cereals, too, were helped by the increase in weeds whose decay helped the nitrogen content of the soil, increasing crop yields. With pasture improving, sheep, similar to Soay and the later Shetland breeds, were kept for meat, milk, skins and the wool which was plucked, though shears are found from the later Iron Age. Spindle whorls, loom weights and weaving combs show that clothes were woven, often, it is suggested, into tartan patterns. Croft Ambrey had pigs which could root in nearby woods, while the very fertile soil around Sutton Walls supported cattle, similar to Dexters, which provided milk, meat, leather and hides. Manuring and crop rotation also helped to increase crop yields. Evidence suggests that wells were sunk to provide water for penned animals, and hay meadows gave winter feed. Some lowland farms enclosed by banks and ditches, though not as large as those of the hillforts on higher land, have been found through aerial survey but many more, sited to use the fertile soil along river valleys, are likely to be hidden by subsequent alluvium. Others will lie under modern farms, or await discovery in future years of aerial survey.

Considering the number of settlements, and the probable size of the population, it is odd that proportionately so few burials have been found. There are some burials in disused storage pits in southern British hillforts but nothing resembling the cemeteries on the Continent. Other Late Iron Age burials had special, maybe princely, status. Perhaps most people were cremated and their ashes scattered in rivers. The decapitated skeletons found in the ditch in Sutton Walls, whose friends evidently could not return to give them the customary rites, have an especial poignancy.

In the later Iron Age large nucleated settlements, often called *oppida* in south-east Britain, started to be built as powerful bases for increased trade by river and sea with the Roman world. The nearest to Herefordshire is the tribal centre at Bagendon, near Cirencester. It seems likely that, by this time, the Herefordshire area was under the control of the tribe known to the Romans as the Dobunni.

Bach Iron Age Hillfort
This hillfort, covering nearly 11 acres, is in the foreground and is situated on the southern end of a ridge of high land, within the confluence of two streams. The photograph looks south-east towards Uphampton Hillfort and beyond that to Westington Hillfort. None has been excavated but they are sufficiently near to each other to imply a possible connection. Many of the field boundaries can be traced on the tithe maps.

Two typical Herefordshire hillforts — Sutton Walls (top) and Wall Hills, Ledbury (below)

Sutton Walls, one of the few excavated hillforts, is a univallate hillfort (i.e. with one ditch and associated bank) with a single enclosure and two original entrances. Finds here included pottery from the Malvern area. Although farming was mixed, more than half the animal bones were cattle, ideal for the surrounding lush grassland. The 36-acre Wall Hills, Ledbury, has two enclosures with two original inturned entrances.

Much of Sutton Walls has been destroyed by quarrying and subsequent infilling with waste. Prior to this, excavation established that occupation was renewed in the Roman period when the site seems to have been a farm. Also found were parts of twenty-four skeletons thrown into the ditch. Decapitation was a Roman execution method and these may have been the last defenders of Sutton Walls who faced the overwhelming might of the Roman army.

The green field left, above centre, is part of *heneage*, 'old homestead and enclosure'. This unusual field-name may have referred to the land holdings, perhaps palace, of King Offa.

It is difficult to decide whether extensions are earlier, later or contemporary with the apparent main hillfort enclosure here at Wall Hills, in the centre of the photograph. The high single rampart, with a trace of counterscarp bank, and ditch of the smaller enclosure, above centre, suggest that this was the last area of the hillfort to be used and defended. However, only excavation could determine the relationship between the two enclosures.

Roman and 12th-century pottery sherds have been found in the hillfort, and two 17th-century cannonballs from the Civil War.

British Camp and Herefordshire Beacon

Low winter sunlight picks out the impressive earthworks of this great contoured Iron Age hillfort which lies curiously close to the equally large Midsummer Hill along the natural boundary ridge of the Malvern Hills. Recent work by English Heritage suggests that the Shire Ditch, on the ridge top left of centre, was originally Bronze Age and was incorporated into the outer ramparts of the two hillforts. Herefordshire Beacon covered 32 acres, with perhaps three enclosures and probably four original entrances. Again, it is difficult to know the sequence of these enclosures — was the hillfort enlarged, made smaller, or both at different times? Artefacts found have included flints and sherds of pottery; the Malvern area supported a thriving pottery industry in both the late Iron Age and Roman times. It is possible hut sites may be identified as in Midsummer Hill where they can be seen as flatter, rectangular areas on the interior slope.

A visually confusing factor here is the renewed use of the site in the Medieval period. A Norman castle, dated to the 12th century, was built at the highest point and the ringwork, known as the Citadel, can be seen centre right. One or more of the earlier enclosures no doubt served as a bailey. Then in about 1287 Gilbert de Clare, Earl of Gloucester, the 'Red Earl', renovated the Shire Ditch to form a boundary between his estates and those of the Bishop of Hereford, after quarrels over hunting rights. It became the county boundary between Herefordshire and Worcestershire.

Aerial photography is particularly useful in the investigation of hillforts. All these aerial photographs show that the layout of such large sites is most clearly seen from the air. The relationship between the component banks, ditches, entrances and various enclosures can be appreciated, and although a 'dead area' will exist in oblique photographs this is reduced to a minimum. In contrast, there is no position on the ground where a complete view can be obtained; even standing on the highest interior rampart will only reveal parts of a hillfort.

Gaer Cop

The soilmarks shown in this photograph complete the evidence for the rampart and ditch still traceable in field boundaries (see tithe map and caption below). The only traces of a standing bank and ditch are in the trees below the road, right. The other fields are intensively cultivated, most recently for potatoes.

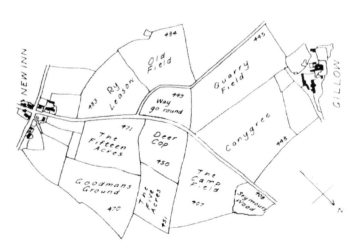

Direct comparison can be made with the defences of this unexcavated hillfort sited on what is now superb farmland and the Hentland tithe map of 1841/1842. The A4137 road bisects the hillfort, which is now heavily eroded by arable cultivation. Beyond the curve of the road, left, above centre in the photograph, the minor road, which can also be seen on the map, follows the old ditch round the field *Way go round*. The dark line of the ditch showing as a soilmark and a cropmark, left, can be seen to contour this high point. An outer boundary ditch is also preserved round *Ry Leasow* and, until recently, around *Old Field*. Below the main road *Deer Cop*, a corruption of Gaer (Welsh for fort), and *The Camp Field* preserve evidence of the site probably because the rampart was useful as a field boundary for the later farmers. *Conygree* shows that rabbits were bred here in the Medieval period.

An Iron Age farmstead near Vowchurch
This small, curvilinear enclosure is typical of many lowland Iron Age farmsteads. Only the ditch appears as a cropmark, the bank having been entirely removed by subsequent ploughing. Interior features such as postholes, pits, or roundhouse walls and drainage gullies are for the most part too small to register as cropmarks and therefore escape detection from the air. The area occupied by the enclosure appears broadly similar to that of the modern farm nearby.

Reconstructed Iron Age roundhouses at Castell Henllys in Pembrokeshire
These are typical of the thatched timber buildings found within Iron Age hillforts and rural settlements. The figure shows their substantial scale, 10 to 12 m across. Both smaller and larger roundhouses are found at other Iron Age sites. Note the low walls and the overlapping thatched roof. Smoke from internal hearths percolated out through the thatch rather than from a central hole in the roof.

Enclosure Complex near Pembridge

It is rare for apparent field-boundaries to be associated with cropmark enclosures of this kind in Herefordshire, or elsewhere along the Welsh border. Here, however, and as cropmarks in the surrounding fields, there are clear traces of an organised landscape with ditch-defined fields. These are clearly earlier than the Rowe Ditch, the now wooded bank that crosses them at an angle. In 2003 Herefordshire Archaeology excavated the enclosure ditch, at left, and found Late Iron Age pottery, some made in the Malvern area and similar to that found within Croft Ambrey, in the fill. Above, and so later in date, was Romano-British pottery. This suggests confirmation that these cropmarks show the site of a Late Iron Age or Romano-British farm. This dating evidence is extremely important as this site may now be compared with other similar sites elsewhere.

Enclosure near Rowlestone

This small enclosure near the southern end of the Golden Valley, occupies a slightly raised knoll. In the top photograph the three enclosing ditches show as green marks in the yellowing corn, but are not yet visible in the grass field to the right. In the smaller photograph, taken slightly later in the summer, the ditches are clearly visible as yellow-on-yellow cropmarks in the ripened crop of the field on the left and more indistinctly as green cropmarks in the parching grassland of the field on the right. An entrance gap through all three ditches can be seen at lower left. The outer two ditches are curvilinear, suggesting that they are part of a small Iron Age settlement. The innermost ditch is more rectangular, hinting at later adaptation in the Roman period.

This example shows that no single episode of photography is likely to reveal all about a cropmark site. One must fly repeatedly throughout the summer, and in succeeding years, to catch each field at its optimum time for cropmark development.

Enclosures near Wellington

These three cropmark enclosures lie alongside the modern A49 from Hereford to Leominster. The shapes of the foreground and most distant enclosures would be consistent with an Iron Age date. The far enclosure is poorly defined in the nearly ripened crop (see thumbnail below to help locate the enclosures) but was seen as a clear cropmark, green on yellow, earlier in the same summer and in previous years. The middle enclosure, wedge-shaped and very precisely drawn, is a puzzle as to date and function. Its further ditch overlaps, and is probably later than, the ring-ditch of a probable Bronze Age barrow, though this is not visible on this occasion. Earlier photographs also show the dark line across the field, centre, continuing across the next field to join the line of the road to a farm to the right of the picture, suggesting an earlier road. The dark pits and narrow lines right of the nearest enclosure may be contemporary with this enclosure. Some of the lines may be geological or former field boundaries, while a pair of lines across the corner of the modern field in the foreground may be the side-ditches of a road.

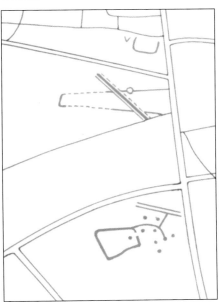

5 The Roman Period

After the Roman Invasion in 43 A.D., Britain was occupied, with up to 50,000 soldiers, by one of the world's first efficient, disciplined armies. They were paid in coins. Roman legionaries had daily weapons drill, with field manoeuvres in combat uniform three times a month when, carrying full campaign kit, they had to march 20 Roman miles, approximately 22 modern miles, in five hours. This intensive training resulted in a force that responded instantly to commands given in battle. Iron Age people were fearsome in the first rush but no match for a force who could change tactics at a given signal. Pacification of Britain took about 35 years but once achieved the very presence of such an army largely preserved a peace that allowed prosperity to develop. Most if not all hillforts were abandoned, the huts within Croft Ambrey and Midsummer Hill hillforts were burnt, and only farmers used Poston and Sutton Walls.

The army built both temporary or 'marching' camps, sometimes for as little as a single night, and permanent forts. Both, being typical playing-card shapes, can now be easily identified when seen from the air. One of the earliest in Herefordshire is the 64-acre marching camp at Brampton Bryan, shown to be probably 1st century A.D. from the additional defence of a *tutulus*, an extra length of bank, opposite its south gate. The latest fort to be discovered, at Blackbush, Abbey Dore, is also dated from before 80 A.D. to judge by its pottery. Other forts include those adjacent to the Roman settlements at Stretton Grandison, possibly Roman *Eposessa*, and Weston-under-Penyard, Roman *Ariconium*, the latter seemingly linked to the iron industry of the Forest of Dean. Others were at Clifford, Clyro, Kentchurch, Tedstone Wafer and a group around Leintwardine, Roman *Branogenium*. Also near Leintwardine the Romans re-used Brandon Iron Age hillfort as a supply depot by building a granary, probably for local grain. A further six forts are suggested by field-names, such as *chesters*, derived from Old English *ceaster*, derived from the Latin *castra*, which in post-Roman times was applied to the ruins of Roman stone-and-tile buildings and walled towns or forts. Another *chester* is Kenchester the only Roman settlement proved to have had a wall around it.

Military sites were built for strategic reasons and the most visible survivals of this are the roads, at least initially laid-out by army surveyors and constructed by the army. Built to last, perhaps requiring little maintenance, many continued in use for centuries, becoming the foundations of modern Herefordshire roads.

In the photograph opposite, part of the rectangular defences of the Roman settlement at Stretton Grandison / Ashperton can be seen in the foreground just left of the bend in the modern road. The settlement has been tentatively identified as the Roman town of Eposessa mentioned in the 'Ravenna Cosmography', a late copy of a Roman map. A Roman fort, probably for a 1st century auxiliary unit, lies north-east of the settlement, which itself is bisected by the A417, a road that overlies the line of the original Roman road from the Roman settlement near Dymock to Much Cowarne and the north-west. Roman roads were constructed in straight sections, with drainage ditches on either side, the lines of which can sometimes still be visible. Here the modern road bends away from the straight line of the Roman road, whilst even the line of the old road has taken on a 'wavy' appearance, perhaps as travellers bypassed sections which had fallen into disrepair.

Roman roads formed very convenient parish boundaries when these were laid out in the 8th or 9th centuries A.D., as between Shobdon and Kingsland, Eardisland and Monkland and Eaton Bishop and Madley. Where a road, later called *straet* by the Anglo-Saxons, ran to a bridge which was swept away in winter floods and not rebuilt after the Roman period, the route had eventually to deviate. The top paving or

Roman road and settlement, Stretton Grandison (opposite)

Roman Fort and temporary camp at Buckton

At least five Roman forts and marching camps, of different dates, have been discovered by aerial photography around the Roman town of *Branogenium*, modern Leintwardine.

Buckton is interesting as it has a temporary camp whose single ditch can be seen above the playing-card shape of the fort's bank, ditch (green) and internal roads (yellow) as the crop begins to ripen. This camp could be from an earlier campaign, but may equally well be a camp of leather tents and timber used while the stone-and-timber structures of the permanent auxiliary fort were being built alongside. Excavation evidence shows that when first constructed, possibly around 80 A.D., the fort had a turf rampart and timber gateways but that these were replaced by a stone wall in the early 2nd century. By 140 A.D. the Buckton fort was dismantled, as were many others. The army required fewer scattered garrisons as the local population became used to the Roman way of life, ensuring a period of peace, the *pax Romana*, a time when trade and commerce could flourish.

gravel surface of the disused section might be robbed but the foundation would remain and even though grass-covered is still noticeable in a pasture field as a firm area for walking, or for cattle to lie on. Such foundations are visible as cropmarks in the ripening grain or parched grassland of the present day. An approximate Roman road map for an area can be made by examining known Roman roads and *street* fields. Stretton Sugwas, originally Stoney Stretton, was thus 'the village along the Roman road'.

Towns provided markets and for the first time farmers all over Britain could exchange surplus produce for coins, which would be saved to buy goods like the local Severn Valley pottery and luxuries such as metal tableware or the beautiful shiny red samian pottery from Gaul, modern France. Coins could even pay for remodelling the dining-room by having underfloor heating with a mosaic floor complemented by painted walls and ceiling, perhaps ordered from *Corinium*, modern Cirencester. In Herefordshire, the local farmers with the best soil took advantage of these commercial opportunities, becoming more and more 'Romanised'. Stone-and-tile rural villas, perhaps with central heating, became fashionable, being preferred to the former timber houses. Known civilian sites include Adforton, Bishopstone, Blackwardine, Donnington, Hentland, Huntsham, Lugwardine and Wellington. New Weir, a villa or riverside trading site by the River Wye in Kenchester Parish, can be visited and Roman walls seen. Putley has a villa site, with a second site beneath the church. A late Roman Christian community may be indicated by the name *eccles*, or *eckley*, originally a church building or a Christian community. Kenchester is one of seven parishes where this name can be found. It is likely that some Roman villa sites could be preserved under churches as one room may have continued for worship when the rest of the house went out of use. Other field-names which are worth investigating as possible Roman sites include *blacklands, coldharbour, cinder, castlefield, port* or *porch, -wardine, ford, wall* and *camp* though most *camps* in Herefordshire are Iron Age sites.

Improved farm equipment included scythes for hay-making and, by the late Roman period, a plough which turned the sod, particularly useful on the heavier soils of north Herefordshire. Romanised farmers simply improved on Iron Age practices. About 400 plants, including chestnut, were introduced to Britain by the Romans, initially for medicine but then for more general food, like peas, lettuce and turnips, and herbs as flavourings. Plants like nettles, imported as a vegetable and to help prevent hair thinning, became established, as did apples and pears which were later to become of particular importance for Herefordshire. Anyone who travelled to the sumptuous villas of the Gloucestershire Cotswolds, or the Governor's palace near Stroud, to have been entertained in elegantly appointed rooms and formal gardens, would have been suitably impressed. Such opulence was probably unknown in rural Herefordshire but agriculture continued and the surviving plants and roads show that Roman Herefordshire was quietly thriving.

Roman and present-day Leintwardine

Although Leintwardine may originally have been a military site all the excavated evidence suggests a civilian settlement. Whatever its earlier history, its people had access to good soil, and it became a town from about 160 A.D. As *Branogenium* it is mentioned in the 'Antonine Itinerary', a copy of a Roman road guide which shows convenient stopping places probably for the Imperial messenger service, the *cursus publicus*. Indeed the excavated bathhouse, where an altar inscription was found in 2001, appears to belong to a *mansio*, an inn. The town's location probably places the settlement somewhere near the boundary of the descendants of the Iron Age tribes of the Cornovii and the Dobunni.

The Roman town had a regular shape, suggesting it was at least laid out by surveyors trained by the army. The modern A4110 bisects the Roman town, whose outline can be clearly traced in field boundaries on the 1847 tithe map. There must have been a timber bridge on the road south of the town across the River Teme. The road, now known as Watling Street, on the east side actually runs in the Roman ditch. The gardens of the houses fronting this on the west side of the road, rise steeply to lie over the rampart and the north-east corner of this can still be seen in the photograph, above right of the church. The chancel of the Church of Saint Mary Magdalene also rises steeply on steps and must overlie this rampart or another substantial feature. Excavations within the town have yielded evidence of buildings and Roman pottery.

Castlefield Roman Fort, Kentchurch

Aerial photographs of this fort, on the interestingly named Castlefield Farm, show that it occupies the same piece of ground as the cropmark of an earlier, smaller, wide-ditched enclosure set at a different angle. It is possible the earlier enclosure was an Iron Age farmstead.

Excavations across the line of the fort's defences showed that it was built either in the reign of the Emperor Claudius, or that of Nero who died in 68 A.D. There was evidence of two periods of timber buildings and the finds included samian pottery and coins. The lower left corner of this fort can often be seen as a shadow site from the B4347 Skenfrith-Grosmont road. The upper right corner of the fort, in the dark area left of the farm buildings, has been destroyed by quarrying which is represented by darker green patches (as identified on the thumbnail sketch below).

A fort had been suspected in the area for many years as they were built at regular intervals along the roads initially constructed by the army to facilitate the movement of troops. However, the exact location of this fort was a surprise as the line of a road, presumably somewhere along the side of the valley of the River Monnow, has not yet been traced.

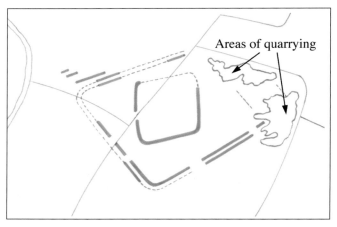

Areas of quarrying

The solid red lines on the thumbnail sketch indicate the lines of ditches that can be readily seen on the photograph above, the dotted red lines indicating the presumed lines of ditches.

Kenchester Roman Town and road to Hay-on-Wye

The Roman road bisecting the kite-shaped town of *Magnis* in the foreground continues a line that can still be followed along the so-called 'Roman Road' north of Hereford, where parts of the drainage ditches may be seen. Indeed, excavations ahead of the Roman Road Improvement Scheme in 2004 found that the preserved Roman road lay partly under the modern country road. In this photograph the road runs west into the background towards the Clyro fort at Hay-on-Wye.

The parchmark of the road is often so clear inside *Magnis* that its dimensions can be measured. Although the interior roads were laid out in a grid, the perimeter defences of *Magnis* were irregularly-shaped, suggesting that the town originated in ribbon development to cater for the needs of travellers, including the constantly moving army detachments, only later acquiring its enclosing defences. Nevertheless, it became important for the local community and may have been the administrative centre for the region. A north-south road, perhaps from Leintwardine towards Monmouth, may have originally by-passed *Magnis* to the east of the town. Roads were crucial for pacification and for trade, although the recent translation of a complaint on one of the Vindolanda tablets from Hadrian's Wall shows that roads were not always kept in pristine condition!

Roman Town of Magnis, Kenchester

This photograph was taken in poor light as rain approached which would have 'washed away' the parchmarks. Nevertheless, the internal roads, building foundations and the wall, where it is not beneath the modern hedges, are clearly shown as parchmarks in the grass.

Kenchester, Roman *Magnis*, was a small, irregularly-shaped, town of 22 acres bisected by the main east-west road from Stretton Grandison to Clyro. It was mentioned in the 'Antonine Itinerary'. Of the three fields it was later divided into, *22 The Walls* had visible masonry. As with all Roman civilian sites, it has excellent farmland around it. Its people had an enviable lifestyle being used to mosaics — two of which are now on the wall of Hereford Museum — wall plaster and pottery, including imported samian tableware. Coins show that this was a trading centre in a market economy and an oculist's stamp, for eye ointment, shows that some quite sophisticated services were available. Other finds include tiles, a bronze ox-head and a re-used milestone inscribed RPCD (usually read as *Res Publica Civitatis Dobunnorum* referring to the town as the regional capital of the Dobunni). The main internal road had a central drain which is clearly visible as a dark line in the photograph.

The town lasted for 400 years, despite a fire in the 2nd century, easily long enough to become a significant centre for the whole locality. However, times became uncertain for the first earth-and-timber defences were later rebuilt in stone, still visible under the hedge by the road. The west gate was partly blocked in the 5th century. This photograph, from 1995, shows, for the first time, a very large building, in the top right of the site, apparently in its own compound, which could have been for administration. This, and the wall, suggest a special function for *Magnis*. Perhaps the town was a collection point for the *annona*, the tax, often in corn, used to victual the army. Other Roman sites are known nearby, including at New Weir which may have been a river port for goods brought up the River Wye, which was navigable this far at that period.

This reconstruction drawing is firmly based on the evidence obtained from aerial photographs and selective excavation. Such drawings help us to visualise something of what it was like to actually live in Roman *Magnis*.

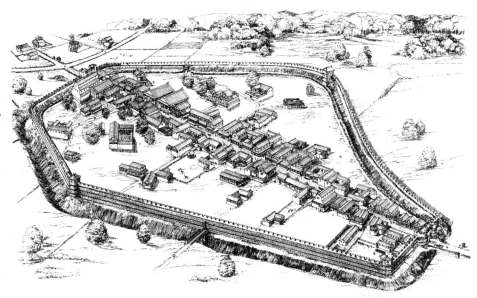

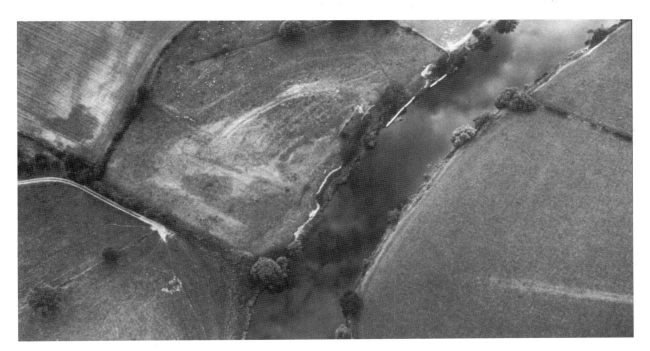

Roman river-crossing south of Kenchester

Running south from *Magnis* to the River Wye the line of the Roman road is visible as a parchmark entering the photograph at lower right. The Romans probably built a bridge of timber which, at times, would have needed an army detachment to guard it. The cropmarks of an irregularly-shaped enclosure, with a straight side and entrance gap, can be seen, left, south of the river. Within it the parchmarks above the wall-lines of a small rectangular building, divided into rooms, can be seen, showing a building which may perhaps have housed the soldiers serving the guard post. Between this and the line of the road are dark areas representing the sites of quarries used to obtain material for the road, with another quarry site on the left of the photograph. South of the river the road line was retained as continuous field boundaries, becoming the still-used 'Roman Road'.

Brampton: a possible Roman Villa

Although this is a precisely defined but fairly wide-ditched enclosure with a centrally placed entrance in one side, its regularity does not *prove* a Roman date. However, it does suggest the possibility, especially if compared to similar excavated sites like Lea Cross in Shropshire, surrounded by a ditch, or Gatcombe, south of Bath, where a villa and outbuildings lay within a rectangular walled enclosure. Nevertheless, assigning a date to features from cropmark evidence alone is risky as rectangular enclosures in many parts of Britain have been shown to date from pre-Roman as well as Roman times. Systematic fieldwalking may provide corroboration if pottery and other dateable artefacts are found but excavation is the only way to prove such speculative dates with certainty.

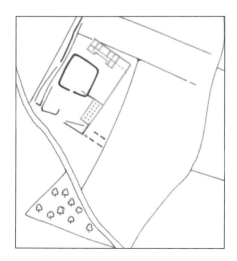

Roman villa at Ashford Carbonel, Shropshire

Just beyond the Herefordshire border, this winged Roman villa and aisled barn (in red) were mapped by the Royal Commission on the Historical Monuments of England from air photographs taken in 1994. It was the square enclosure (black), around 35m across (about half the width of the Brampton enclosure), which first caught the eye of the air photographers. In this case, however, the differing alignments of the villa and enclosure suggest that they are of different dates, the enclosure perhaps belonging to an iron Age rural settlement which was later succeeded by the Roman villa.

Possible Romano-British farmstead near Eardisland

A complex of regular and irregular enclosures like this on farmland near Eardisland is often considered to show a British farm in the Roman period. That there was farming near to this site in the Arrow Valley, in the area around Eardisland, Pembridge and Staunton-on-Arrow, during the Roman period has been confirmed by the 2003 excavations centred on Pembridge. Apart from British pottery, imported samian was found, indicating a farming market economy based on selling surplus crops and animals that allowed the purchase of luxury foreign goods. Other investigations have shown possible deforestation linked to agricultural intensification and re-organisation of the landscape. It is even possible that the present field pattern originated at this time. Certainly this air photograph, by identifying the existence of a settlement in Eardisland which has otherwise vanished from the archaeological record, suggests that there is far more to discover in the whole area.

6 Mercia

The Herefordshire area was a long way from the lands initially plundered and then settled by groups related to the Anglo-Saxons and it took several generations before the area became part of Mercia. Indeed, river names and some place-names, such as Dinedor, Moccas, Tretire and Treville, continued in the British language. Leominster's British, or Welsh, name was *Llanllieni*, referring to the minster, which was a central or 'mother' church. Nevertheless, changes did happen as centralised Roman-inspired order broke down. Though people may have continued to live in the former Roman settlements they no longer functioned as administrative and trading centres. Trading and markets declined so there was less incentive to grow surplus food, most people becoming self-sufficient. It is likely that some land reverted to waste, used for common grazing of cattle and sheep, perhaps under scattered trees. Woodland increased, and was managed by coppicing and pollarding. Skills in using stone, for roads and buildings, were no longer needed as timber structures were preferred.

The survival of Christianity is a clue to life in this troubled period. Church dedications such as those to Saint Dubricius, reputedly born in Madley in the 6th century, show that Celtic traditions were strong and enduring. Monastic foundations, as at Hentland, are known. A few churches, including those at Acton Beauchamp, Bredwardine, Eaton Bishop, Kilpeck and Lower Brockhampton have traces of possible Mercian / Anglo-Saxon masonry. The herringbone masonry at Edvin Loach Old Church also suggests a similar origin. Minsters founded in tribal centres served scattered churches in huge parishes. The minster church at Leominster was probably the shire's most important ecclesiastical centre, a status either shared with, or supplanted by, Hereford. Sites of other important churches included Bromyard and Ledbury.

Although field-name evidence suggests a Roman presence in the Leominster area, the traditional story of the origin of the town lies in the foundation of the nunnery. The story describes how Merewalh, variously described as King of Mercia or of the Western Hecani from *c.*650 to *c.*680, was converted to Christianity by a priest from Northumberland. As a result, in *c.*658/660, he built a nunnery, endowing it with land around the site. Merewalh's son was the Mildfrith who was said to have built Hereford, and one of his daughters was Saint Mildburga, Abbess of Wenlock. Interestingly, Merewalh's name means 'famous Welshman', suggesting that these people west of the Severn were the indigenous population. The nunnery seems to have achieved great prestige in the 10th and 11th centuries; according to the Domesday Book the royal estates around Leominster were held by Queen Edith, wife of King Edward the Confessor and sister of Earl Harold Godwinson, who later became King Harold.

The end of the nunnery was the result of a scandal based in the tangled politics of the time. In 1046 Earl Swein Godwinson, elder brother of Harold, was returning from a military expedition against the South Welsh. Swein abducted Eadgifu, Abbess of Leominster and lived with her for a year. They may have had a son. Eadgifu's plight provided a useful pretext to dissolve the nunnery and Swein's sister, Queen Edith, certainly benefited. However, the minster continued to operate. In 1139 it was refounded and rebuilt as a Benedictine Abbey by monks from the Abbey of Reading, who had been given the manor in 1123 by Henry I. The abbey became famous for its sheep. When in 1539 it was dissolved, the church was retained for parish use.

The greatest survival of British names in Herefordshire was south of the River Wye in an area which became Archenfield, the name possibly derived from Roman *Ariconium*. The Wye, which originally bisected a much larger area of Archenfield, eventually became its eastern border and the area

Offa's Dyke near Lyonshall

From the Saxon historian Asser's comment that Offa built a dyke 'from sea to sea', it is believed that this bank and ditch ran from the estuary of the River Dee to the confluence of the Wye and Severn, a distance of about 177 miles. However, south of Kington the surviving lengths of dyke are often short and intermittent, making it difficult to trace its exact course. This section of dyke is to the west of Lyonshall, marked by the line of trees running up the photograph.

remained in the Welsh Diocese of Saint David's until the 19th century. The earliest Anglo-Saxon kingdom was north of the Wye and the tribal name of the Magonsaete, or Magonsaetan, may have been taken from Roman *Magnis*, which became part of the royal estate around Sutton. Although there may have been a small Roman settlement guarding the ford across the Wye, Hereford as a town was founded under Magonsaetan rule, probably by Mildfrith, and it became a new religious centre with a minster. Traditionally the first bishop was Putta in 676 A.D. and a later bishop was described by Bede as ministering to the peoples west of the River Severn. The original territory of the Magonsaetan was the area now occupied by central and northern Herefordshire and South Shropshire, while the Hwicce were probably south of this — now the present-day extent of the Diocese of the Bishop of Hereford. The most famous bishop was Cuthberht who became Archbishop of Canterbury in 740 A.D., while two later bishops each served for more than 40 years.

When the area became a part of the larger kingdom of Mercia, a palace may have been built immediately south-west of the old Sutton Walls Iron Age hillfort. Traditionally it has been associated with King Offa, who ruled Mercia in 757-796 A.D. and was sufficiently powerful to claim to be *Bretwalda*, or overlord, of all the English. The centre of Offa's power was at Tamworth and Lichfield, but it was at Sutton that Aethelberht, King of the East Angles, was said to have been murdered in 794 A.D. The legend describes how he had arrived to marry Offa's daughter, only to be beheaded by an agent of Offa's wife, an event now depicted on the west front of Hereford Cathedral. A statue of Aethelberht can be seen in the Cathedral, his eventual burial site. On the same gravel terrace as the Cathedral, a common religious choice of site, by the River Wye was Saint Guthlac's monastery, which also seems to have been founded in the 8th century. It is possible that the enclosure around a manorial site east of Sutton Saint Michael church was first built in the late Mercian / Anglo-Saxon period and if so this would be an extremely rare and important find.

Life was hard in these post-Roman centuries before the Norman Conquest, with fighting between the Welsh and English, Viking raids, and struggles for land between neighbouring groups. Gradually the area of Herefordshire became more 'English', and by the time of the Domesday Survey of 1086 the majority of place-names were of Anglo-Saxon origin, with over a third ending in '-ton', denoting a farm with an enclosure. The uncertain times demanded defences and these can be seen in the plan, and the later 10th-century revetment, of Hereford, the earliest of the *burhs* or fortified centres, where a mint was established as the only one west of the River Severn. Hereford's Row Ditch, the bank defending the River Wye crossing, visible south of the river, may originally have been part of the *burh* defences. However, despite these defences Hereford was plundered in 1055 by a combined force of Welsh and English factions. The Cathedral, which had been re-built under Bishop Aethelstan in the 1020s-1030s, was burnt. Undoubtedly devastated by these events, Bishop Aethelstan, already blind, died soon afterwards. Reprisals were undertaken by Harold Godwinson who added the area to his lands.

Enclosing land with a bank and ditch — which can survive as greenways — was already traditional but the defence of property was now vital. Probably the oldest boundary in the area is the dyke south of Yatton

Rowe Ditch, Pembridge: a cross-valley dyke

Rowe Ditch looking north, seen as continuous field boundaries, centre. This Rowe Ditch is one of the 'short dykes' of broadly the same period as Offa's Dyke, forming cross-valley or cross-ridge boundaries, ending in dense woodland, probably to protect cleared farmland by acting as 'forward defences' against the Welsh. Certainly, these boundaries, large enough to survive for many centuries, were clearly meant to be deterrents. Excavations in 2003 suggest that Rowe Ditch was imposed on the landscape, crossing the existing field pattern, in about 650 A.D., whereas the 8th-century Offa's Dyke seems to follow the field pattern.

Wood near Ross, which may even have been a tribal boundary of the Magonsaetan. Other boundaries are known, such as those at Kings Caple and Acton Beauchamp, which may also be Mercian / Anglo-Saxon. Territorial boundaries occur elsewhere in Britain but the most famous is Offa's Dyke, built in the 8th century to define the western border of Mercia. Although other Early Medieval dykes are known, this was the longest in Britain. Variations in building technique suggest that it was built in sections by different gangs of men, as shown on Rushock Hill, near Titley, where two sections meet at an awkward angle. It seems to have been a negotiated border with the Welsh and so was not apparently required through Welsh-influenced Archenfield. Indeed, only six miles of the dyke survive in Herefordshire. That the ditch, or dyke, was the border rather than the bank is shown by a section in Lyonshall, which was still a significant field boundary in 1840. Here, three fields are called *Row Ditch* while another is *647 Offa's Ditch Meadow*. Whilst field boundaries may follow the line of the Dyke, parish boundaries rarely do so, indicating perhaps that some of them follow older boundaries.

Mercian *burh* in central Hereford
The perimeters of the late 9th / early 10th century *burh*, or fortified centre (shown with a dashed white line in this picture) were eventually bounded by the line of present day Victoria Street, West Street, East Street and Mill Street. Within this area of about 50 acres the later Medieval street plan is largely preserved by the modern roads. Excavations showed that gardens of the houses in Cantilupe Street lie over the 10th-century rampart, which has been exposed in one garden. The line of the Norman defences are marked by the modern ring-road.

Leominster

The Priory Church of Saint Peter and Saint Paul, with central Leominster beyond, stands on the site of a much older nunnery. The trapezoidal precinct of the minster, enclosing approximately 150,000 square yards, can still be traced as indicated in the sketch (right). It was bounded on the north by the Kenwater, on the east by the River Lugg and by a great earthen bank and ditch on the west and south, parts of which survive. The Pinsley brook was dug in the 12th century for fresh water and drainage. Not all the monastic buildings were demolished and those below the church became the Leominster Union Workhouse in the 19th century, then the Old Priory Hospital and finally offices of Herefordshire Council. The tunnel for the former abbey leat, used for water, still runs beneath part of the complex.

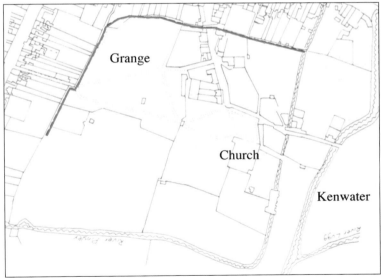

The sketch above shows the priory's *Vallum monasterii* marked in red, indicating the western and southern extent of the minster's precinct (orientated here to align with the photograph), showing it enclosing a stretch of present Church Street and the buildings to its south.

Bredwardine church

Although much restored, the church is thought to be mainly Early Norman. However, it has herringbone masonry, enormous lintels and uses tufa, which possibly suggest Mercian / Anglo-Saxon work. The church is now famous as the burial place of Rev. Francis Kilvert, who was the incumbent from 1877-1879. 'Kilvert's Diary' is a marvellously detailed account of 19th-century rural life. The white Vicarage was built in 1805, the field-name for which, *485 House buildings and Pleasure grounds*, supports Kilvert's lovely descriptions of the garden, which may be the site of the c.1200 castle vineyard.

Churchyard and deserted village at Acton Beauchamp

The restored Church of Saint Giles at Acton Beauchamp has a 9th-century Mercian / Anglo-Saxon carved cross-shaft re-used as a lintel for the tower doorway, suggesting an earlier church on the site. Indeed, the earliest charter reference is dated 716 A.D., when King Ethelbald of Mercia gave *Actona* to Saint Mary's Abbey in Evesham. By the 1086 Domesday Survey the manor belonged to the Bishop of Bayeux, later owners being the Beauchamp family, hence the final name. In the photograph a walled garden is prominent behind Church House, built in 1802. The intriguingly named *168 Hope Meadow*, centre and right, shows the holloways and house platforms of a deserted Medieval village, with a line of fishponds against the modern road.

Pre-Norman enclosure at Sutton Saint Michael

The mainly Norman church at Sutton Saint Michael, centre right in some trees, is double-celled, suggesting that it incorporates an earlier church. In the field adjacent to the church, by the flooded River Lugg, is a massive drainage ditch apparently running from the river across the field. Between this and the church another shadow mark of part of a rectangular enclosure can be seen and it seems that the soilmark in the ploughed field in the foreground is related to this. Tradition associates the area with King Offa and the site of his palace is suggested to be south of the nearby Freen's Court (see p.73). However, establishing that

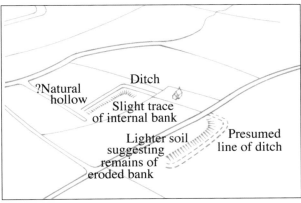

features are Mercian / Anglo-Saxon is notoriously difficult as the pottery of this date was not fired to a very high temperature and so is friable in Herefordshire soil. Pottery is one of the most reliable ways of dating sites. Indeed, in 2004 a radiocarbon date was obtained for a puppy crushed in the foundation slot beneath the palisade that supported the turf bank of the enclosure. This suggested a building date centring around 1050 A.D., in the reign of the Saxon King Edward the Confessor (1042-1066). Nevertheless, the position of the church and the nearby enclosure may suggest earlier site occupation.

Recent excavations here have revealed a complex of structures, the earliest feature being a ring-ditch. Later structures were found to be Medieval and a demolition date for the earlier buildings in the late 11th century was obtained. The site was probably that described in the Domesday Book as being the specialised royal estate administrative centre for the harvest from the king's manor at Marden.

7 The Middle Ages

After his victory at the Battle of Hastings in 1066, William the Conqueror claimed ownership of all the land in England. His experiences of treachery in Normandy led him to avoid allocating compact estates to even his chief supporters and the component manors were divided between many shires. These lords in turn followed the same cautious policy. Tenants were required to perform feudal duties for their immediate overlord. The manor peasants, as well as providing labour on the lord's own *demesne* or home farm, had to pay dues such as when a son inherited or a daughter married.

The troubled Welsh border was tightly controlled. Known as the March, it had three power bases in Chester, Shrewsbury and Hereford, whose lords had virtually independent fiefdoms. Herefordshire had been one of the first areas of England to be influenced by the Normans as Edward the Confessor appointed his Norman relatives and friends to positions of power in the county, and they built three pre-Conquest stone castles: Ewyas Harold, Hereford and Richard's Castle. After 1066 William fitzOsbern was created Earl of Hereford and constructed further castles at strategic points, such as Clifford and Wigmore, and refortified Ewyas Harold, to subjugate a population who had to provide the labour force. He began the process of building planned boroughs, defended by castles, whose laws were Norman in contrast to the ancient customs of the area. These centres provided markets, which attracted trade, had a huge influence on the surrounding areas, and signified that the Normans were indeed an occupying force. The Romans had used the same method with their own towns.

The first castles were all built as mottes, usually with one or more baileys, or as ringworks, quickly erected by local people forced to help in the construction. The Bayeaux Tapestry shows a motte, or mound, being built in layers and excavated mottes do show layers of stones which were essential to support the weight of a timber tower, or keep. That mottes were built for great stability explains why so many still exist, especially along the Welsh border. A ditch, or moat, was usually constructed around the motte and a further ditch with internal bank and timber palisade, often surrounded one or more embanked baileys packed with living quarters, hall, chapel, kitchen, stables, workshops and other storage facilities. A few motte-and-baileys even utilised existing Iron Age defences, as at Herefordshire Beacon. Banks radiating from hillforts, as at Midsummer Hill, may also belong to this period, suggesting cattle enclosures. In larger castles an internal efficient water supply was essential for self-sufficiency and, if necessary, to withstand a siege.

Many villages and hamlets, especially in west Herefordshire, had a motte-and-bailey castle, which gave the Norman owner a strong operations base for swift control of the land and people. More than five times as many mottes are found in west Herefordshire, facing Wales, than in the eastern part of the county. Designed to be easily garrisoned by a few men-at-arms, they also had to accommodate the lord's retinue on periodic visits or when local trouble erupted. Some castles in pacified areas remained in timber, gradually falling into disrepair. Others, guarding strategic roads, passes, river crossings, or particularly fertile areas, were soon replaced in stone, but even these were only heavily garrisoned when necessary. Castles like Clifford, Goodrich, Kilpeck, Longtown, Weobley and Wigmore, dominated the countryside. Their presence was usually enough to ensure compliance, though terror tactics could be used, as in the 13th century when Roger de Clifford seized the Bishop of Hereford in his own cathedral and imprisoned him for three months in Eardisley Castle.

The ruthless border magnates were from a few inter-related families such as Bohun, Braose,

Richard's Castle (opposite)

Clifford, Lacy and Mortimer. During the Barons' War, 1260-1266, Prince Edward, later King Edward I, was helped to escape from Hereford Castle by Roger Mortimer who fought with him at the Battle of Evesham against Simon de Montfort. Wigmore Castle was the Mortimer power base and it was a later Roger Mortimer who made Queen Isabella of England his mistress and hanged Hugh Despenser, King Edward II's lover, in Hereford market place. A descendant of the family, by marriage of the Mortimer heiress into the family of York, took the crown as King Edward IV. Henry Tudor's victory at Bosworth in 1485 ended the Wars of the Roses and brought the new King Henry VII the enormous estates of the defeated Yorkists, supplanting the power of the border lords. He was able to instigate a new system of government and Ludlow Castle was used to host the Council in the Welsh Marches. The times of relative peace encouraged the building of manor houses, usually sited near to farmland, though many in Herefordshire were still provided with a moat which could at least slow an attacker.

All Herefordshire's present day towns were founded or extended during the Medieval period. Hereford Castle was linked by a wall to the new borough, whose core was the old Saxon *burh*. In the 1086 Domesday Book Hereford is already described as a city, Wigmore as a borough, and all the other later towns as agricultural manors, Leominster being the largest. Bromyard, Ledbury, Kington, Ross and Weobley were well sited to become local markets, though their later prosperity did fluctuate. Domesday also gives us the first opportunity to meet Herefordshire people, providing

Nant-y-Bar motte, Dorstone
One of a string of mottes built in strategic positions along the English-Welsh border, Nant-y-Bar stands on a spur overlooking tracks through the foothills of the Black Mountains. The substantial motte, surrounded by a deep ditch, has traces of walls suggesting that it was sufficiently important to have been rebuilt in stone.

names, though admittedly principally of the landlord class.

However, not all the planned towns were successful. In the photograph of Richard's Castle (on p.50) the original motte, top right, dates from *c*.1050-52, in the reign of King Edward the Confessor (1042-1066). It was probably built by Richard, a Norman, the son of Scrope, or Scrob, a name which shows the Scandinavian / Viking origins of the Normans. The strategic position chosen for the fortification is evident. The castle, mentioned in Domesday, was strengthened and rebuilt in stone in the 12th and 13th centuries. Its extent is preserved in fieldnames such as *Castle Meadow* and in *Castle Bank*, the lower part of the field in the centre. Right of centre is the Church of Saint Bartholomew, whose separate tower of *c*.1300, when it was a part of the defences, dates from the very end of the castle's period of importance. Interestingly, of the forty separate church towers in England and Wales, seven are in Herefordshire, suggesting a need for an easily defended refuge as well as a lookout point. Just below centre in the photograph, below the castle and the church, is the triangular market place, bordered by the road, of this deliberately planned borough, further defined by a boundary bank. In 1216 King John (1199-1216) granted a charter for a weekly market and an annual fair. Castles attracted traders and could develop the economy of an area. However, the importance of Richard's Castle declined as Ludlow and Wigmore became more administratively useful.

Chanstone Tumps, Vowchurch
Situated in the fertile Golden Valley, the most prominent of the two Chanstone Tumps, a typical Herefordshire name for a motte, is clearly defined as *419 Tumulus* on the tithe map. There is evidence of foundations on the solidly built, flat-topped tump. The two tumps are divided by the River Dore, delineated by the trees, and it has cut into the main earthwork over the years. The almost-levelled second motte, above the trees, is marked by the left of the three bare areas.

Cusop Ringwork
The stone-built bank clearly shows as a shadow site, whilst earthworks within the ringwork suggest the foundations of buildings. Although restored, the Church of Saint Mary, in the trees to the left, dates from the Norman period and was certainly contemporary with the castle.

Newton Tump, near Clifford

This tree-covered motte with very well defined D-shaped bailey surrounded by a slight bank and ditch lies in *1391 Court Meadow*. A recent geophysical survey suggests further structures, even perhaps a chapel, above left. There is evidence of stone foundations on the motte and of walls in the bailey bank. The fieldname, which may originally have been Welsh *cwrt*, meaning a court or mansion, supports this having been a substantial and important site, similar to Chanstone in being low-lying.

Pont-hendre motte-and-bailey, Longtown

Pont-hendre is Welsh, *pont* being bridge, and this is where the road crosses the Olchon Brook, south of Longtown. *Hendre* denotes a winter dwelling, used with the *hafod*, or summer dwelling on the higher pastures, in the system of transhumance. The very substantial, high, motte is clearly seen, left, with the typically crescent-shaped embanked bailey between the mound and the tree-lined Olchon Brook. Though the defence capabilities were undermined by the fact that the fields, upper left, could actually overlook the castle, this would have been overcome by the height of the tower on the motte.

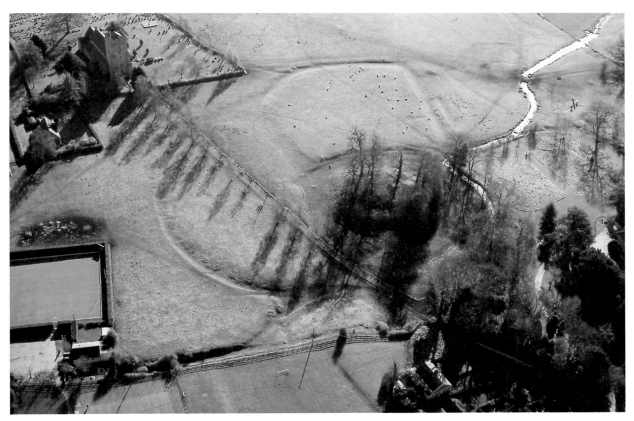

Kingsland Castle

Kingsland Castle is a site with a motte and multiple baileys. The earthworks of the motte, centre right (and see thumbnail sketch below), crowned by trees and surrounded by a wide ditch, has two baileys, beyond and to the left, separated by a depression. Traces of ditches suggest the possibility of a further enclosure or bailey extending beyond the left-hand edge of the picture. The motte has the stone foundations of a probable shell keep. Kingsland means the royal estate in *Leen*, a Welsh district name denoting streams, and the meadow adjoining this site was *Merwold Croft* until the 19th century, presumably after Merewalh, ruler of the Magonsaetan in the 650s A.D., who is said to have had a palace here. Certainly, he reserved the area for himself when he endowed the nunnery in Leominster with land and this probably accounts for its name. The later castle was sufficiently well appointed for the tradition to be feasible that King John stayed here in 1216. The late 13th- / early 14th-century Church of Saint Michael stands top left.

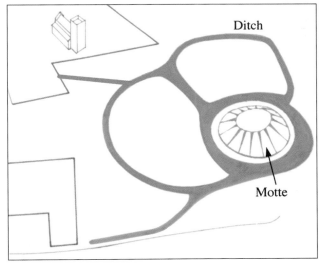

It is becoming clear that the whole area of the Arrow Valley sustained a large population in the Medieval period. It was by no means an 'empty' landscape which must have made it traumatic for the local people when one of the decisive battles of The Wars of the Roses (1455-1485) was fought here. The 1461 Battle of Mortimer's Cross, fought over a wide surrounding area, resulted in the accession of the Yorkist claimant as King Edward IV (1461-1483) and Kingsland has a monument to commemorate it.

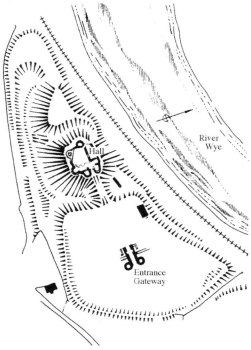

Clifford Castle

Clifford Castle (with plan opposite), built by William fitzOsbern, stands right on the border, the green field right of the river being in Wales. Mentioned in Domesday, Clifford was a site of major importance being termed a *castlery* and having a borough. It guarded a possible incursion route. The huge motte and surviving masonry of the keep, a hall with an undercroft, two storied gatehouse towers and three other towers, dominated this strategic point on the River Wye. Stone defences enclosed half of the original bailey and the excavated barbican can be seen centre, in the brown field, with the lower part of the field being the outer ward enclosed by a bank. The castle is traditionally thought to have been the home of Jane, or Joan, Clifford, Tennyson's 'Fair Rosamund', mistress of King Henry II (1154-1189). The north-west tower is now called Rosamund's Tower. Members of the powerful Clifford family were buried in Dore Abbey, where an effigy can still be seen. The castle was destroyed by Owain Glyndwr in 1402. It is possible here to see the well cut, good quality, ashlar used for the exterior walls and the rubble-based interior walls, the bonding being lime mortar. Excavations have recovered pottery, a bullet mould, iron nails, a knife, arrowheads, a key and a bridle bit.

Longtown Castle

The photograph shows clearly why it has been suggested that Ewyas Lacy, later Longtown, was a Medieval castle set within a Roman fort, though the Roman connection has not been proved. The line of trees shows the apparently typical 'playing-card' shape of a Roman fort (see also thumbnail sketch to the right), the Medieval castle bailey occupying the right-hand quarter of this area, with traces of walling and a gateway to the upper left of the motte, on which the round keep still stands, centre right. The burgage plots of the borough follow the line of the ridge to the south-east, top left. Between these and the castle was the market place with the 13th-century Church of Saint Peter.

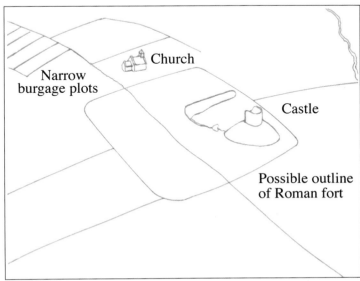

The round keep was the very latest design in 1215-1223 when its builder, Walter de Lacy, Sheriff of Herefordshire, was responsible for the county's defence against the Welsh. He may have paid for it by raising a loan from Hamo of Hereford, one of the wealthiest financiers in England. Interestingly, the track on the west of the castle, outside the curtain wall at centre right, is called Jew's Lane, perhaps commemorating Hamo.

Goodrich Castle

The huge, expensive and impressive castle of Goodrich, the best preserved castle in Herefordshire, faces Walford, the ford of the Welsh, across the River Wye. Standing on a crag of red sandstone, it dominates and controlled a major route, probably used from at least the Iron Age. Excavations to the south, in part of the field at top right, revealed an early Christian cemetery. Thought to have been first fortified by Godric of Mappestone, the oldest part of the castle now visible is the wide, dry, rock-cut moat. All the masonry is firmly built into the rock, adding to the castle's strength. The oldest surviving structure, *c.*1160, is the grey stone keep, centre, built of conglomerate probably brought up river from the Forest of Dean. Square, three-storied, faced by ashlar and originally entered from the first floor, the keep's size can be gauged by the visitors standing its summit. The 13th-/ 14th-century circular towers round an inner ward, the great hall, kitchens, gatehouse and semi-circular barbican of red sandstone glow in the sun. The chapel in the gatehouse has been partly furnished to give the modern visitor an idea of the original appearance of such a room.

Until the 15th century the castle continued to be refurbished, becoming the property of the Talbot family, later Earls of Shrewsbury. Then, in 1646, the castle was besieged during the Civil War. Held by Sir Henry Lingen for King Charles I (1625-1649), it threatened communications between Gloucester and Hereford. The Parliamentary forces, under Colonel John Birch, whose effigy is in Weobley Church, determined to capture the fortress. After one abortive attempt 'Roaring Meg', a specially-cast mortar carrying a two hundredweight cannon-ball, was used in the bombardment, causing enormous damage especially to the water cisterns. This, combined with mining operations, brought about the surrender of the garrison, whose lives were spared. The castle was then deliberately slighted to prevent its re-use.

Wigmore Castle

Wigmore Castle, standing on the spur end of a hill, is superbly impressive when viewed from the east, dominating the north-south route that was first metalled by the Romans. The original motte-and-bailey castle, built by William fitzOsbern, lay west of the church near the burgage plots of the borough. It was later moved further west to a new commanding site in what became *Castle piece*.

By Domesday, Wigmore was in the possession of Ralph de Mortimer, whose often ruthless descendants, by power politics and judicious marriages, managed to hold Wigmore until the 15th century. In 1191 the new castle was besieged and captured by William Longchamp, Justiciar to King Richard I (1189-1191), because Roger de Mortimer supported Prince John and plotted with the Welsh. It was then strengthened, though in 1264 Simon de Montfort also took it. After his defeat at the Battle of Evesham, Simon's head was sent to Maud de Mortimer.

That Wigmore was not only a strong power base, but was also expected to provide comfort, is supported by the South Tower having at least three heated rooms. It was sufficiently well appointed for the greatest in the land to visit and tournaments were held, the most magnificent being in 1330 when Roger Mortimer was ruling England, with Queen Isabella, in the name of her son, the young King Edward III (1327-1377). Edward asserted himself shortly afterwards and Roger, first Earl of March, who had once escaped from the Tower of London, was executed on the site of Tyburn, London. Below, and north-east, of the castle was a rectangular enclosure, bisected by the present road and now only traceable as cropmarks. This was probably the site of the tournament ground and may later have become a deer park.

At the start of the Civil War, the Harley family held Wigmore. As late as 1643 it was described as the strongest castle in England but Sir Robert Harley could not afford to repair two castles and so it was dismantled in favour of Brampton Bryan. Later, part was sound enough to be used as a prison but eventually it became a stone quarry. Recently, it was consolidated as a 'romantic ruin'.

Added to the great shell keep, started in the 12th century on an enormous motte, top centre, were 13th- / 14th-century towers, curtain wall and gateway, bottom right in both pictures. A vaulted cellar survives and the amount of rubble can be gauged from a doorway in the curtain wall buried almost to the top.

Wigmore Moor, further north in the valley, was a lake with Wigmore Abbey on a promontory. Approaching the castle from the north-west it would have been seen reflected in, and enhanced by, the lake water and looking truly awesome. Visible prestige was everything.

Moated site at Whitbourne Court

Constructing a moat around your house was, for those who could afford it, a way of providing a degree of protection, the larger and more perfectly formed the moat, the wealthier the owners. By the 15th century moats were built less for defence, but more as ornamental garden features in a planned landscape.

Whitbourne, a manor of the Bishops of Hereford, was converted to a country house, centre, by Colonel John Birch after the 17th-century Civil War. Now Georgian, it retains some of the 15th-century Bishops' Palace. Behind the house was a 7-acre pleasure garden where, in the tenure of Bishop Richard Swinfield, 1283-1316, fruit, peas and beans were also grown. The water-filled moat, which contained fish and eels, used to completely surround the manor as there is reference to a drawbridge. The River Teme is top centre. In the trees to the right of the house, is the Norman Church of Saint John the Baptist with later modifications, the house, bottom right, having subsequently been built as the Rectory. The field above the Rectory is called *Day Lawn*, indicating that there was a park here. Other facilities are indicated by *562 Brewhouse Orchard*, right, and *552 Church Yard Orchard*, bottom left. There was also a vineyard and rabbit warren, yet further evidence that this moated site was an important seat of the bishops.

Moated site at Lower Brockhampton

Lower Brockhampton is in a secluded valley north-east of Bromyard. The 1,700-acre estate, with traditional farms and woodland, belongs to the National Trust and is open to visitors. The photograph shows the early 15th-century house, centre, a lovely example of timber-framing, probably built by John Dumulton, then lord of the manor. Between the house and the farm to the right is the gatehouse, also timber-framed and built a hundred years later. Its deep shadow can be seen. Above the house is the moat, full of water, which now does not completely enclose the site. A further, smaller, square moat, also full of water, is under the trees, top left, surrounded by orchards. Far too small for a garden, it perhaps once enclosed a dovecote or a summer house. Lower centre is the roofless Norman chapel with 13th-century chancel and walls of tufa, a soft limestone, often found in local early Medieval churches as it was easy to carve. It is curious that it is outside the moat and at a different angle to the house.

Old Court, Bredwardine

Old Court, just below the centre of the picture, with the modern farm lower right, is skirted by a tractor track. The original house was on this square, flat mound, with stone foundations, surrounded by a dry ditch. The name *Court* is still attached to this site, as at Whitbourne, Brinsop, Hampton and Freen's Court, and suggests that this was a prestigious building. Bredwardine Bridge is at the top right. The church [see p.48] and castle, to the south, are on the same side of the River Wye as Old Court. The house would have been of a similar size to the present farm-house, whose core is 14th century, and is a typical Herefordshire house with a cross-passage.

Brinsop Court moated manor house

Brinsop Court is a 14th-century manor house, refurbished by Hubert Astley in the early 20th century, using designs by Henry Avray Tipping. A new wing, lower centre, was added. The original house seems to have been on three sides of the courtyard. The house is in its own valley and is completely surrounded by a water-filled moat, now partly bridged by the entrance driveway, and here seen more flooded than usual. There are also two fish-ponds, top right, separated from the moat by a grass-covered causeway and fed by springs and a stream. On the other side of *42 Moat Meadow*, bottom left, is another small square moated site similar to the one at Lower Brockhampton (see p.60).

Moat at Seed Farm, Cradley

Although the house was re-modelled in the 17th century, it dates from the 16th century or earlier. The moat, averaging two metres in depth, may have once encircled the house. By the 1838 /1839 tithe it had been filled in on the north, left of the house in the photograph, and further filling has continued to reduce its size. The feeder stream is right, above centre, where the right-angle shows it is man-made, supporting the original importance of the moat. It is likely to have been an early defensive feature and provides evidence for the early occupation of this site.

Dinmore Manor and Chapel of Saint John

Dinmore Manor stands on the site of a Chapel of Saint John of Jerusalem, patron of travellers, and its associated conventual buildings. Presumably it was sited to help travellers on the Dinmore Hill road. In 1189, in the reign of King Richard I (1189-1199), it was founded as a commandery, later preceptory, of the Knights Hospitaller of Saint John, an Order dedicated to giving help to pilgrims travelling to the Holy Land. It stands on a platform, in a small, secluded valley with terraces, fishponds and earthworks that indicate the monastic activities. A 14th-century well-head covered a spring and water is now a feature of the gardens. Fieldnames include *Friars Grove* and *Great St. John's Meadow*. The complex included a tithe barn and north of this was a pigeon house, demolished c.1800. The Hospitallers' became very large landowners, with property locally in Herefordshire, Shropshire, Gloucestershire, Monmouthshire and Glamorgan until their Dissolution in 1540.

Part of the north wall of the chapel, bottom centre, is 12th century, while most of the remainder of the building is 14th century. The chapel has interesting features including a tower room thought to have been used by the priests. The chapel was once longer and there was another, perhaps older, building on the north side. The large yew tree below the church is reputed to be over 800 years old. The monastic courtyard was smaller than appears here, though the earliest parts of the late 16th-century manor house, centre right, built by the Wolrych family, probably stand on monastic foundations. Other buildings, further right, were added in the 18th century. The cloisters, left, terminating in the octagonal South Room built by Richard Hollins Murray after he bought the manor in 1927, stand on virgin soil, outside the monastic complex. Their arches use stone from the demolished Hereford gaol, while the interiors are lined with Bath stone. At the same time the Music Room, with the long roof and the stone-mullioned bay window above the cloister, was built of Hollington and Bath stones.

8 Religion and Rural Life

The Normans were great builders and ensured that each village had its own stone church, with brightly painted internal walls where the effigies of successive lords and their families demonstrated continuing power to awe the villagers. Few of these churches survive in their Norman form, most having been added to or heavily restored in subsequent centuries.

Hereford's new Norman Cathedral, staffed by a community of clerks, was finally completed under Bishop Robert de Bethune in the 1140s, while the Bishop's Palace, lower centre in the photograph opposite, with its Medieval hall, was started soon afterwards. The present Cathedral is the result of further re-buildings over the centuries, some to allow devotees to visit the shrine of the second of Hereford's saints, Saint Thomas de Cantilupe. The Cathedral stands in its Close, with the cemetery above, fronting buildings that once housed the canons. A 13th-century house survived as the Cathedral Barn, top right. The decagonal foundations of the Chapter House are centre right, while a corner of the largely 15th-century College of Vicars' Choral is further right, with the 19th-century Old Deanery and other buildings of Hereford Cathedral School above. The new Mappa Mundi building, which also houses the Chained Library, below centre left, stands by the site of an old road, possibly Roman, that once led to the ford across the River Wye, just below the picture.

The Norman lords founded, endowed and patronised monasteries. Medieval monasticism arose from the Rule written by Saint Benedict of Nursia, 480-553 A.D., which was a set of guidelines for a properly regulated monastic life. This was not the only Rule but was the most widely adopted and led to the foundation of the numerous and often wealthy Benedictine monasteries, often located in towns. In Herefordshire the most important was in Leominster. In time it was felt that communities had lapsed from Saint Benedict's strictures and so some monks founded new and more austere houses. The most numerous were the Cistercians, who founded an abbey at Dore in the Golden Valley. Herefordshire's other monastic foundations included the Augustinians at Wigmore, with nuns at Aconbury and Limebrook, the Cluniacs at Clifford, Praemonstratensians at Holme Lacy, the austere Grandmontines at Craswall and the Order of Tiron at Titley. In addition, there were houses of the military orders, the Knights Templar and Hospitaller, and of the Franciscan and Dominican friars. Plants cultivated for food, or medicine, can still be found on some sites and monastic fishponds often survive.

Domesday had noted that the Welsh border had oxmen to control plough teams. Cattle were stronger and more economical than horses as they could be eaten when no longer used for ploughing. Good horses were far more valuable for transport. Oak trees, valuable for timber, were also planted to provide shelter, allowing cattle to stay out in most weathers. Increased farming efficiency, and so more food, must have helped the population increase between 950 and 1150 A.D.

The technique of ploughing using 'ridge-and-furrow', which maximised drainage and so saved at least part of the crop in wet conditions, had started under the Anglo-Saxons. The technique became a characteristic of Medieval farming and was employed on the ancient scattered plough fields of the dispersed farms as well as on the very large open fields in which most villagers had strips. Herefordshire appears to have had both systems, with the smaller, older fields mostly surviving in the west, very reminiscent of the *bocage* in Normandy.

In the 16th century John Leland noted how 'enclosed' Herefordshire was, with few large open fields. However, the open-field system was in use mainly in the central plain. Field-names like *Upper Field*, *Middle Field* and *Lower Field* are clues for the earlier existence of the two, or three, open-field

Hereford Cathedral (opposite)

system of rotation, with each huge field growing the same main crop. Most parishes also had a number of small fields, divided into strips, each with a common crop that may have included barley, spring-sown oats on poorer soils, leeks, peas, beans, vetches and rye, with autumn-sown wheat and fruit on the best soil. The field pattern shows that most communities were scattered, with small village centres around the churches.

Hedges were important. 'Dead' hedges were hurdles used as temporary barriers. 'Quick', or living, hedges grew crops of berries, fruit, nuts and timber. Fences and hedges were forbidden under Norman Forest Law which applied to Dean, Treville, northern Archenfield, Malvern, and smaller areas in Madley and Much Cowarne. Forests were not continuous woodland so villagers within the areas had to use 'corn ditches', ditches with earth and stone banks, to protect their crops from deer. Over time encroachments or 'assarts' were made in the woodlands; four are mentioned in Domesday for Herefordshire. In the 12th century Robert of Ewyas gave the monks in Ewyas Harold land to assart. Later, Dore Abbey was given permission to 'till, assart and enclose', the term 'enclose' involving building a dyke around an area and then ploughing it. Field-names like *stocking* indicate assarts, whereas *ley* indicates woodland grown for up to six years to replenish the soil after cereal use.

In the 14th century and later this progress was halted. The climate changed, becoming cooler and wetter with longer icy winters, and brought harvest failures, animal diseases and starvation. This was compounded by the Black Death which reached Britain in 1348, after which plague continued to recur sporadically. Carvings of the 'Green Man', the image of the greenwood, appeared in churches all over Europe in an attempt to ward off the evil; local examples are at Dore Abbey, Hereford Cathedral, Bosbury and Ludlow. The population of Herefordshire was probably halved and some villages were abandoned. Many such deserted Medieval villages, or DMVs, can be seen as grass-covered platforms, the sites of former houses, lying alongside the wide sunken trackways of the former village roads. Sometimes the church is still standing in isolation or with a farmhouse, whose oldest section is the sole survivor of the village houses. Income from rents dropped so land was used for sheep and many of Herefordshire's half-timbered buildings, along with the market halls in Ledbury and Pembridge, were paid for with profits from wool.

The Dissolution of the Monasteries resulted in the estates of the abbeys, priories and nunneries being broken up and acquired by royal supporters. These houses had long been a source of a meal for the very poor, an employer, and the regular bells would have provided a time reference for those living nearby.

Wigmore Abbey
This site was possibly the fifth move for these Augustinian canons after their first local foundation at Shobdon in about 1140. Building started at Wigmore in 1172 and the abbey was dedicated in 1179. It was destroyed, apart from the church, by the Welsh in the reign of King John, being rebuilt c.1379. At the 1538 Dissolution most of the church was destroyed though the Mortimer vault, housing many generations of the family, may survive. Roger Mortimer IV, executed at Tyburn in 1330, was buried here.

The present house stands, under snow, on the line of the western range of the abbey which ended right, at the site of the church where parts of the walls still stand. The garden marks the cloisters while the frater, or dining-room was to the left. The eastern range was in the field below.

Craswall Priory

Craswall Priory, half-hidden to the left of the farm buildings is in a most remote location, at the head of a secluded valley, where one of the headwaters of the River Monnow rises, surrounded by the rough pastures of The Black Mountains. Founded c.1225, one of only three foundations in England of the Order of Grandmont, its patron was Walter de Lacy, whose castle was at nearby Longtown, then called Ewyas Lacy. The church was small and plain, reflecting their austerity. With no distinction between the few choir monks (originally hermits) and lay-brothers, clothing was cheap rough sackcloth with brown wool hooded scapular, woollen gaiters and leather shoes. They were allowed to collect land rents, most being sent to the French mother house. The priory was dissolved in 1441.

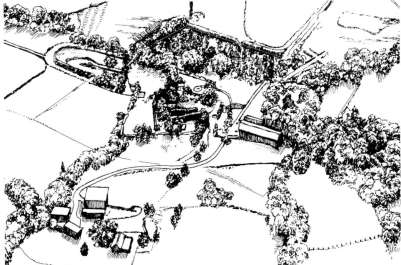

Although vegetarian, with no animal herds, the monks did have fish-ponds, here shown with the typical rounded end at top left, made long and narrow by damming a stream. Only an air photograph can show such a complex confined within its outer precinct wall, outlined in red on the drawing. The remains of the church itself are roughly in the middle of the precinct, on the left of the track.

Almeley Church and Castle

The Almeley Church of Saint Mary (above), built in the 13th and 14th centuries with a tower started in about 1200, probably stands on an earlier site that formed a complex with the Norman motte-and-bailey castle to its right. Although there is another motte in the area, this motte's importance is indicated by the field-name, *520 Court Orchard*. The bailey, lower centre, is straight sided. Fishponds, top right, essential to provide fish on Wednesdays, Fridays, Saturdays, on feast days and during Lent, were also a mark of status.

Old and new churches at Edvin Loach

The abandoned Old Church of Saint Giles, in the foreground, is considered to be early Norman in date. Partly built of tufa, it has herringbone masonry which is a frequent feature of Mercian / Anglo-Saxon structures. In the trees just beyond the present church, is a Norman motte, the bailey covering the churchyard.

The site is an incredible palimpsest. The field beyond the churchyard is *18 Upper Camp*, with *20 Lower Camp* off the photograph bottom left. The fieldname *Camp* is often associated with Iron Age hillforts and the topography also suggests that the church stands within a hillfort. Roman pottery, including samian and Severn Valley ware, has been found by systematic fieldwalking in *Lower Camp* field. There were also finds of Medieval pottery. The 19th-century Church of Saint Mary, centre, therefore stands between the Norman motte and the Old Church with its possible Saxon connections, in an area used by the Romans, all probably within an Iron Age hillfort.

Orcop Church

The Church of Saint John the Baptist at Orcop has a tower whose weatherboarded upper part has a truncated pyramid roof with a bell stage and spire, supported inside by large posts. The church is 13th century in date with 19th-century restoration. It stands in a square churchyard with its spacious former vicarage alongside.

Ganarew Church

The 19th-century Church of Saint Swithin was built on the site of an earlier church, probably that of Monmouth Priory's 12th-century Chapel of Saint Thomas (probably Becket). The churchyard has a curious, semi-oval shape. By tradition Vortigern, who is said to have invited the Saxons to Britain, is buried here.

Deserted Village, Lingen

The motte, centre left, of Lingen Castle and the earthworks of the square bailey with a pond, above the motte, are thrown into relief by low winter sunshine. The wide track, centre, and associated ditches to the right of the motte belong to a deserted or shrunken Medieval village. In Domesday this was one of the manors held by Ralph de Mortimer who had estates in twelve English counties. His tenant at Lingen took his name from the village and a canon from Wigmore Abbey ministered to nearby Limebrook Nunnery, another Mortimer foundation.

Little Dilwyn

The road curves towards a tributary of the Stretford Brook running across the photograph and around a pond and an island, all of which are in *1596 Mill Meadow Building etc.* This indicates the site of a former mill and mill-race. There is a dried-up rectangular moat beyond the pond, which was not recorded before this photograph was taken. The field, centre and to left of the farm, has clear earthworks, and the complex appears to be that of a previously unrecognized deserted Medieval village. The farm buildings have been in the same position since the 1837 tithe map.

Kilpeck: castle, church and deserted Medieval village

Originally the 12th-century church, under trees above centre, was dedicated to Saint David, probably a local Celtic Saint Deui / Dewi, and the castle's chapel to Saint Mary. The church now has the double dedication. Its circular churchyard, possibly some masonry, and its alignment survive from the earlier church. The extension to the graveyard is the square, above centre right, which was excavated before being used for burials. It extends into the inner bailey of the castle, pointing towards the motte, built by Norman de Plies or his son, which still has parts of the shell keep that was added later. The outer bailey, which may have been the garden, is beyond the motte on the right with remains of a dam for fishponds at top right. Another outer bailey is to the top left of the castle, bordering the modern village. By 1211, when King John made the first of three visits, the castle must have been well appointed. Left of centre is a road, lined by trees, which is approximately on the road of the deserted Medieval village. To the left of the church on a bend in the road is the triangular area of the market. There are traces of the village houses in the two fields on either side of the tree-lined road, though the earth-works are more easily seen in the right-hand field around which the outer village boundary can also be traced by the hedge-bank. The fields beyond the road on the left are all named *Priory*, preserving the site of the precincts of the cell of the Benedictine abbey of Gloucester (now Goucester Cathedral) endowed by Hugh fitzWilliam / Hugh de Kilpeck in 1134. Kilpeck Priory suffered later financial difficulties being exempted from taxation in 1419 because it was so poor. The decline of the village and castle in the 14th century may have been linked to the famines of these years and to the Black Death, which reached Herefordshire in 1348 / 1349.

A notable feature in this picture is the circular feature which can be seen crossed by the field boundary just above centre on the far right. This may be geological but could alternatively be a Prehistoric enclosure.

Field Lynchets, Lingen

This site, on a slope near Lingen, shows lynchets and narrow ridge-and-furrow in the centre foreground.

Lynchets form as the result of terracing across the contours of a slope. Occasionally this may have been deliberate, but if so crop yields from the terrace would have been seriously affected as the inner part of the terrace cut into the less fertile subsoil. This was a serious consideration when the alternative to a good harvest was starvation. Far more likely is the formation of terraces over time.

Stones needed to be removed from a slope before the ground could be tilled. These would be used to provide protection, from animals, for the subsequent crop by building dry stone walls around the plot of land. As the ground was worked so the loosened soil imperceptibly moved downhill until stopped by the lower wall lying across the contours. Soil slippage occurs at an angle of more than 45 degrees. Soil would infill the gaps between the stones and vegetation would take hold on the lower side eventually covering and holding firm the wall, thus forming a lynchet. It is suggested that the formation of some lynchets could be as early as the Bronze Age, while others are centuries later. Here, the only relative dates are given by the boundary hedges, centre, which overlie the lynchets, showing that the lynchets are older.

Narrow ridge-and-furrow can also be seen, centre foreground. It is suggested that the width of the ridges and associated furrows can help determine their last date of use, with narrow ones being later than the wide ones more characteristic of the Medieval period.

Ridge-and-furrow fields near Freen's Court

Typical ridge-and-furrow fields seen to advantage under a light snowfall and low winter sunlight. Freen's Court, which stood at top left until demolished in 1957, was built in the 15th century just above the flood plain of the River Lugg, seen winding from top left round to bottom right. The defender of Goodrich Castle in the Civil War, Sir Henry Lingen, lived here. The house had a moat (no longer visible), and, in the 17th / 18th centuries a water garden was created with rectangular pools separated by gravel paths. They can be seen above centre left and in the field, *73 The moats*, below this. The pools cut through older ridge-and-furrow ploughing.

Ridge-and-furrow was formed by a heavy plough turning the soil right over. A furrow was ploughed in one direction and then a second parallel to it in the opposite direction. The third furrow was ploughed next to the first, the fourth next to the second and so on until the ridge formed by the sods always being turned inwards was the required width. Medieval ridges are usually about five metres across and are often in the shape of a reversed S. Later ridges are narrower and straighter. A 'headland', a higher unploughed area where the plough-team turned and where soil could be cleaned off the plough share, can often be seen where the ridges end. Occasionally ploughed-out ridge-and-furrow can still be seen as soilmarks due to the comparison between the light-coloured ridges and the darker organically rich topsoil which slipped into the furrows over the centuries of use. Here they are shown as shadow marks in winter sunshine after a light snow-fall.

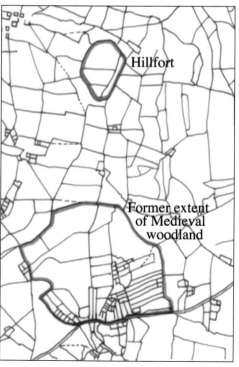

Hillfort

Former extent
of Medieval
woodland

Ancient woodland at Edwyn Ralph

In the foreground are the surviving traces of an ancient wood which originally covered most of the area. There is evidence as far back as 3800 B.C. for coppiced poles used in the construction of the Sweet Track in the Somerset Levels. This shows that woods were being managed to obtain desired lengths. Ash and wych-elm coppice easily but if animals are likely to browse the tender new shoots pollarding from the top of the trunk was the preferred method. Wood provided rods, poles and logs for fences, wattle-work as in wattle-and-daub, and for fuel. The particularly valuable timber from tree trunks could be sawn into planks and beams for houses, barns and boats. The woodland floor and the brashings provided animal bedding, forage for pigs and attracted game. Woods were carefully used and were highly prized.

Looking along the line of the ridge in the photograph from Edwyn Ralph into Thornbury, the field system, here under snow, can be seen to follow the topography. In the foreground is the surviving ancient woodland, named on the tithe as *145 Edwin Wood*. The curvilinear shape of Wall Hills Iron Age hillfort, notable for having a largely undamaged original entrance, is top centre. The continuous hedge-line running from centre right towards the hillfort is a trackway that since it follows the ridge could be very ancient, perhaps even from the Iron Age.

Rabbit breeding at The Warren, Willey

This area at The Warren is just inside the county border, north of Presteigne, and is a typical example of the heathland warrens common all over Britain, in this case now used for sheep pasture. When rabbits were introduced to Britain in the 12th century by the Normans, for their fur and delicious meat, they apparently needed help to breed. It was also convenient to group the burrows so the rabbits could be easily found. 'Pillow mounds', man-made burrows named for their shape and comprising soft earth thrown up from a surrounding ditch, were used. Here there are two examples, centre and left (shown in solid

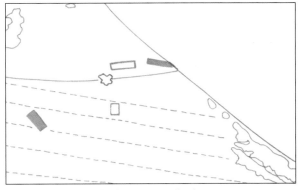

red on the accompanying sketch). Larger areas, often bounded by a bank and ditch, came to be known as a *warren*, a name which came to refer specifically to rabbits. Other breeding areas can also be traced in field-names by *coney*, an old name for a rabbit.

Between the pillow-mounds are two house platforms (shown in red outline on the sketch). Medieval long-houses in Herefordshire often had the lower courses of wall made of stone with the rest of the walls being in wattle-and-daub, woven poles covered by mud, straw and manure to render the building water-tight. People lived in one end and the animals in the other. When a longhouse decayed, perhaps after about 30 years or more, it would be levelled and a new structure built on the firm level area. Over the years this resulted in the ground-floors being raised in comparison with the tracks outside. When the houses finally ceased to exist, the house platforms will have usually remained and can be mapped to show the layout of a farm or village.

Medieval pillow mounds were common and many have survived in hillforts. They can be seen in Wapley Iron Age hillfort, where in the 18th century the Harley family of Eywood continued rabbit breeding by walling the whole hill to use as a huge warren. Two of the three pillow mounds there are clearly seen on the photograph on page 22 and on the front cover as oval features. The centre one has been recently used to help adders breed.

9 Rural Economy and Country Estates

Once the Welsh border was peaceful, Herefordshire was no longer in the political and military front-line. It was famous for 'wheat, wool and water' according to William Camden, at the end of the 16th century, but the problem was access. Travelling was difficult. In 1622, William Laud, later Archbishop of Canterbury, wrote to his friend John, Viscount Scudamore of Holme Lacy, the restorer of Dore Abbey, complaining bitterly about the state of the roads near Ross. Laud had landed in a muddy ditch. Indeed parts of the county were so remote that Roman Catholic recusants were able to live unmolested.

There was a resurgence of trouble during the 17th century Civil War when Hereford was besieged and changed hands as control alternated between the Royalists and Parliamentarians. People experienced opposing armies foraging off the land — polite terminology for taking what they wanted! Many of the gentry were involved, sometimes with different family members on opposing sides, but most tended to have moderate political views. Local men did volunteer for the armies but this was more out of a need to overcome poverty than out of conviction. Otherwise, if you could keep your head down, and your goods hidden, you could survive with your livelihood intact.

There had always been outside contact through trade but what started to change in the 16th century was the attitude of the landowners to farming and the idea of private property. Working the land was still considered a communal affair as it was very labour intensive — until people were replaced by machinery in the 19th and 20th centuries — but starting in the 16th century, country landowners wanted to maximise their profits. Such efficiency often took little notice of the plight of the people involved, for some villages were simply cleared to make way for more sheep. The result of such 'improvements' was that Elizabethan England had more beggars than ever before. Indeed, Rowland Vaughan, one of the first of

Herefordshire's improvers, showed, to his credit, that he was aware of the employment problem when he claimed that his waterworks scheme in the Golden Valley could provide desperately needed work for 2,000 people, probably an exaggeration, engaged in forty-eight trades besides farming.

Rowland Vaughan described his scheme in a book published in 1610 and claims to have started his waterworks in the 1580s, evidence surviving in a main trench and attendant sluices on the side of the Golden Valley between Peterchurch and Chanstone, along with two mills. The system allowed the ground between the main trench and the River Dore to be flooded in the early spring, and again in April for a first hay harvest in June. Flooding raised the ground temperature, encouraging early grass growth. If cattle were not grazed then two further hay crops could be cut. Other water meadow systems can be detected at Hampton Court, Holme Lacy, Kingsland, Risbury, Shelwick Green (see page 7) and Staunton-on-Arrow.

Herefordshire continued to rely on sheep, the native breed being the Ryeland, a small, white-faced, hornless sheep, whose short staple high-quality wool commanded top prices in Europe. The flocks were fed on the aftermath, what was left after rye had been harvested, and to protect them from cold weather were kept in sheepcots, covered pens that could take up to three hundred animals. The slight foundations of these can be found in pasture fields but such practices have also left traces in field-names. The quality depended on the feed and the breed continued longest around Ross where the sandy soil, unsuitable for wheat, was used for rye. Hemp, flax, parsnips and turnips were also grown. The area, extending into Gloucestershire, was known as the Ryelands. The popularity of the breed declined when, in order to capitalise on the rise in mutton prices caused by the Napoleonic Wars, the Ryeland was crossed to increase its size and fed on turnips, reducing wool quality.

Berrington Hall (opposite)

Cattle had always been important for ploughing. Herefordshire villagers were poor and their animals had to be hardy, but they were valued sufficiently for groups of farmers and labourers to fight against both sides in the Civil War to protect their crops and cattle. Indeed, 2,000 of these so-called clubmen actually marched on Hereford in 1645 to protest against the plundering of the Civil War armies.

Elsewhere in early 18th-century Britain farming improvements were made by the spread of the Norfolk four-course-rotation of wheat, turnips, barley and clover. In Herefordshire a version of this only worked on the sandy soils around Ross. Fruit trees were often grown in hedges and by the 18th century Herefordshire was considered the 'Orchard of England'. Clover and rotational rye-grass were common and were used alongside water meadows. Turnips were often grown with potatoes — used to feed pigs as well as people — between the rows in the hopyards.

The present Hereford cattle originate in the breeding programme followed over several generations by the Tomkyns, later Tomkins, family of the Weobley area. The breed proved ideal for the American west and exports were also made all over the world, including South America, Africa, Russia and Japan. Most of the farms notable for Hereford cattle were in north Herefordshire and, interestingly, seven of them had belonged to Leominster Priory in the Medieval period.

Pigs had always been important as they could be run in woodlands and provided those that ate them with a fat layer to keep out the winter cold. Bacon pigs were fattened for winter on windfall apples and on the 'must', or 'pomace' that remained after cider production. Cider apples had been introduced by the Normans and became popular especially as cider was safer to drink than water — babies were often baptised in it! Field-names show that nearly every cottage had its orchard, with everyone who could do so making cider and perry, from pears, though not in the same quantities as cider.

Even as late as the 19th century Herefordshire remained a diverse agricultural county, with little industry. Most trades, apart from those needed locally, were related to wool. The deciduous oak and beech woodlands provided timber for ship building, fed pottery kilns like those at Lingen, and provided fuel for the iron forges in the north-west uplands, in the Golden Valley, around New Weir and at St. Weonards. Iron and brick production can be traced in field-names. Lime neutralised the acid clay soils but limestone had to be imported to feed the numerous lime-kilns. Other imports included cheese, Welsh butter and coal. There were close links with Wales and for a long time Welsh was still spoken in Hereford. Local exports remained agricultural. Hops, introduced in the 15th / 16th centuries, were sold in Worcester. Cider went to London, Lichfield, Birmingham and Manchester, though higher prices could be obtained for desert apples that kept well. Ross was a centre for exporting wool. Herefordshire had great potential but trade was impeded by the lack of good communications. The state of the roads was a problem and, though several attempts were made to remove the weirs on the River Wye, it was often the river itself that impeded traffic with its variable currents and volume of water.

Herefordshire's field pattern started to change in the 1700s with Parliamentary enclosure. Evidence from the resulting surveys, and the tithe surveys, show that the gentry were increasing their land holdings, those dispossessed of small fields having to move into the towns or villages. Landowners also built new large houses on their estates. In the 16th century these included Luntley Court, which was the Tomkyns' house in Dilwyn, Hall Court in Much Marcle and Freen's Court at Sutton. Later houses included Weston Hall in Weston-under-Penyard and Holme Lacy, which was altered in the 19th century. Suitable gardens and parks were laid out. Difficulties were ignored and, if necessary, churches, (as at Brockhampton Court and Dulas Court), and even villages were moved. At Garnons the main road to Hay, which followed the old Roman road, was moved nearer the River Wye and sunk so that it did not disturb the view of the river from the house. Landscaping was fashionable and two of the greatest designers, Richard Payne Knight and Uvedale Price were born locally. Humphrey Repton and 'Capability' Brown worked in the area, the latter at Berrington Hall and at Moccas Court where roads were simply closed to create the park. Such estates demonstrated the wealth of the landowning class.

Brockhampton Park, Bromyard

Brockhampton Park is the 18th century country mansion built to 'replace' the old Brockhampton Manor at Lower Brockhampton (see page 61), demoting the manor to the status of a farmhouse. The photograph shows the whole complex of house, outbuildings, formal gardens, kitchen garden and chapel. The house stands on a slight spur, the former site of a farmhouse, The Hill, and is made of brick. The field below the chapel is *11 Brickclamp*, suggesting the bricks were made on site. The main entrance to the house is sunlit, above centre right, and above it is the site of the parterre, a feature of the formal garden. The stables and service courtyard lie to the left of the house. The whole is surrounded by mature trees with the park beyond. In the centre is the elliptical kitchen garden, surrounded by a curved brick wall. Bottom right is *9 Pear Tree Meadow*, which may preserve an older use or may connect with the kitchen garden. The grey-stone chapel in the foreground was built by George Byfield c.1798. It replaced the ruined chapel at Lower Brockhampton, showing how the juxtaposition of main house and church can be traced right through from the Medieval period. The Brockhampton Estate, owned by the National Trust, is pioneering a number of projects relating to sustainable farming. These include an apple orchard survey to assess the potential for cider and fruit juice production and a farm building survey to identify possible new uses.

Berrington Hall, facing page 77, now belongs to the National Trust and was built in the 1780s by Thomas Harley. The architect was Henry Holland, son-in-law of Lancelot 'Capability' Brown, who designed the park and gardens. Berrington Pool (top), with the tree-covered island, formed from a tributary of the River Lugg, was intended as a focal point. The house backs on to a courtyard with the ancillary buildings. These large houses, with their numerous indoor and outdoor servants, were, apart from luxuries, self-sufficient communities. Each had a walled kitchen garden which provided the diverse micro-climate necessary for growing fruit, flowers and vegetables throughout the year. The house and its associated gardens are separated from the park by a ha-ha, a sunken deer fence, glimpsed as a circular line just beyond the house. Some of the layout of the formal gardens can be seen beyond the kitchen garden. Field boundaries, which were removed in the 18th century, show as straight lines across the park. The fields above the trees, top right, are all crofts, or small-holdings, and the old field below the trees, right, is *Pigeon House Orchard*, all indicating a settlement, parts of which were cleared in the landscaping.

Hampton Court, Hope-under-Dinmore

The original Hampton Court, sometimes mistaken in documents for the one in London, was Medieval but was remodelled by Thomas, Lord Coningsby in the early 18th century and by John Arkwright, a descendant of the industrial entrepreneur, in 1830-1850. There is some remaining 15th-century work, including the chapel. James Wyatt was employed to 'gothicise' the house in about 1790.

The photograph shows how great houses were often laid out around courtyards, possibly using foundations of the original building. The conservatory or orangery was re-designed in 1846 by Joseph Paxton, who designed the Crystal Palace for the Great Exhibition in 1850. All the grass areas around the buildings are *Lawns*, reflecting the garden layout leading to the park beyond. If this name has survived from the original Medieval manor then it indicates part of the early park. The walled garden has recently been re-laid as formal gardens, to include a maze and utilising canals, water always having been a feature of such gardens.

This photograph of 1995 shows parchmarks in the grass which appeared following a prolonged drought. They preserve features of the gardens, such as paths and terrace walls, and show successive flower-bed layouts.

Ruined mansion of Eywood, Titley

Two views of Eywood, built c.1705 for Edward Harley, brother of the first Earl of Oxford. The house was later remodelled and then eventually demolished in 1958. Visitors to the house included Lord Byron, Uvedale Price and Richard Payne Knight, the latter said to have been the lover of the then Lady Oxford.

The top photograph shows the straight lines, centre, of an impressive approach avenue, many of whose trees were documented before felling, with traces of terracing and features on either side. It meets the ha-ha around the garden in the centre of the photograph. In the trees, centre left, is the Garden Pool, surrounded by Garden Wood with mature deciduous and coniferous trees. The kitchen garden stands above the house, left, below a square of trees. Below this is the wall of a long orchard. On the other two sides of the trees is a curiously curved field giving a resemblance, perhaps superficially, to the moat at the old Bishops' Manor at Whitbourne Court (page 60). Perhaps this was the site of an older house.

The photograph on the right shows the layout of the now ruined house in more detail. As often happened, it was built around a central courtyard. The north entrance, whose long shadow can be seen in the photograph left of centre, top, and the partially standing outer walls of the main house, are the main survivals. The 18th-century stables and the laundry are also standing. Beyond the entrance, top left, the outline of a semi-circular terraced formal garden can be seen. The octagonal 18th-century pigeon house, which had 760 nest holes is centre right. Another amenity was an ice house. Both of these clearly demonstrate the luxurious lifestyle enjoyed by the family.

Whitbourne Hall, a 19th-century mansion (above)
Whitbourne Hall was built by Edward Bickerton Evans in 1861-1862. Evans, co-owner of the Hill, Evans Vinegar Works in Worcester which sold vinegars and wines, was well travelled and his house is in Greek style. Although the part of the house with the semi-circular bay window is roofless, the remainder has been sympathetically converted into self-contained apartments. The landscape around the house is noted for the redwoods, cedars and firs planted to give a Mediterranean ambience, whilst the modern formal garden has clipped yew hedges.

Moccas Court

Sir George Cornewall rebuilt the house and outbuildings in the 18th century. Moccas Court itself is built in brick with stone dressings partly to a design by Robert Adam. The stables, Home Farm and other buildings are grouped around courtyards screened by a shrubbery and yew trees from the main house. Lancelot 'Capability' Brown was employed to improve the landscape and, later, Humphrey Repton was consulted whilst Richard Payne Knight and Uvedale Price were frequent visitors. The surviving park is amongst the five most important areas of relict wood pasture in England. The terraces to the left of the house lead to the River Wye. Beyond the terraces the outline of the sunken lawn created on the site of a demolished service range can be clearly seen. The whole complex was enclosed by a ha-ha, constructed in 1786.

Treago, St. Weonards

Treago was built by Richard Mynors in the 15th century as a copy of Raglan Castle, seat of his patron the Earl of Pembroke. After a period of neglect it was refurbished in the 19th century when the stable block, lower left, was added. However, the structure of the main fortified house was little altered. The whole area above the stable block, left, is *739 Lawn* which suggests that Treago had a late Medieval park. The bridge, top right, over the Garren Brook is 19th century in date.

10   Yesterday and Today

Transport difficulties led in the 19th century to the development of toll roads, with still visible toll houses, and the building of canals to connect Hereford with Gloucester, and along the Teme Valley to Leominster. As a result the price of coal in both Ledbury and Leominster was halved. Horse-drawn tramways served the Hereford-Abergavenny and Hay-Kington routes.

The first train arrived at Barton Station in Hereford on 28 October 1853. Barrs Court Station, originally surrounded by meadows, opened in 1855 and within a few years there was a network of lines across the county, making an immediate impact. Pontrilas, for instance, at the junction of the Newport-Hereford line and the Golden Valley Railway, became a depot and commercial centre where it was said anything wanted could be purchased. Relaxed attitudes allowed passengers to board at the track-side as well as at halts. In fact most people still lived in the villages, which were largely self-sufficient, the towns with their centuries-old weekly markets providing extra commodities.

In the 20th century Herefordshire was sufficiently isolated to be used for military camps, hospitals and a munitions factory at Rotherwas in both World Wars. In the Great War, The Herefordshire Regiment fought at Gallipoli, in Palestine and on the Western Front. Herefordshire men and women also served as sailors, in the airforce and as nurses in both Wars and every community has its War Memorial.

In the Second World War evacuees, schoolchildren and their teachers, came from Birmingham, Bootle, Crosby, Essex and Liverpool and joined local school-children to help with harvesting, still very labour-intensive, and potato-picking. Gypsies too came regularly for hop-picking. Feeding the country was a priority and much land was brought under the plough. The girls in the Women's land Army and prisoners-of-war were allocated to different farms. Requisitioned houses included Berrington Hall, used as a convales-cent hospital. Whitfield Court became a depot for the Royal Electrical and Mechanical Engineers who left behind the concrete bases laid as tracks for the hundreds of vehicles. It was also selected as a future Canadian Embassy if London needed to be evacuated.

There were numerous army camps, including Hergest Camp at Kington, and airforce bases across the county. The hut bases survive at Foxley, where Polish soldiers were stationed. The runway shows clearly as a cropmark in wheat on the Royal Air Force airfield at Madley, where Rudolf Hess, Hitler's deputy, was flown in June 1942 on his way to prison near Abergavenny. The military presence still continues as Herefordshire has the home base for the S.A.S.

Even greater changes followed the two World Wars. Machinery began to be used on farms, resulting in a sharp reduction in the number of people directly employed on the land. Industries such as Henry Wiggin & Co., producers of nickel alloys, relocated to Hereford, bringing many key workers and families, whilst other industries were either started or expanded. Farms have become larger, more owner-occupied and subsidy-driven. Beef and sheep markets have experienced periodic crises. 'New' crops include reintroduced oilseed rape and linseed. Hops still flourish although on reduced acreage, whilst cider producers have tended to amalgamate. There are still many miles of hedges and the decline in woodlands may have been halted due to set-aside.

Tourists first came in the 18th century, seeking the Picturesque. Now the quality of the landscape is given recognition with the designation of the Malvern Hills, and Wye Valley, as Areas of Outstanding Natural Beauty. Tourism, and the employment it brings is now immensely important for the county.

Herefordshire's smaller towns have also become tourist centres. Despite changes, they still reflect the narrow pattern of Medieval burgage plots, as seen, opposite, in Leominster, with Corn Square towards the top.

Leominster (opposite)

Ledbury: church and market hall

The Norman Church of Saint Michael and All Angels has Medieval additions including the 13th-century tower, now with an 18th-century spire. The church was possibly an 8th-century minster. Ledbury was a manor of the Bishops of Hereford.

The 17th-century timber Market House, foreground, in the wider part of the main shopping street has sixteen massive posts of Spanish chestnut and English oak, probably from Malvern Chase nearby. Standing at the end of what was once the market-place, it is attributed to John Abel, who died in 1694, known as 'the king's carpenter', and is only one of many timber buildings in this attractive market town, many of which line Church Lane.

In the lower foreground are the re-built 19th-century almshouses of Saint Katherine's Hospital, founded in 1231, which has a 14th-century chapel and hall, with an original roof.

Three poets lived here: William Langland, Elizabeth Barrett-Browning and John Masefield, who wrote: 'I know no land more full of bounty and beauty than this red land, so good for corn and hops and roses.' A renowned Poetry Festival is held in July.

Medieval patterns in Bromyard

Beyond Bromyard's market square, lower centre, the bold curve of Broad Street and High Street is echoed by Rowberry Street to its right, where a 16th-century timber house survives. This part of the town clearly shows the original pattern of long, narrow Medieval burgage plots.

The Frome Valley area, around Bromyard and Ledbury, is ideally suited to growing hops which flourish in loam soil with good drainage. Brewing for beer uses cones from the female plants, which can be harvested for twenty years. Tithe maps show hop fields were once widespread in the area and as hop-picking was labour intensive casual workers came regularly from the Black Country and South Wales. Now production is mainly concentrated on a few farms where machinery can harvest economically in larger fields. A Hop Trail has been devised which begins at Bromyard Heritage Centre housed in an 18th-century stable block in Rowberry Street, where there is an exhibition on hop growing.

The famous Bromyard Gala in July has a variety of country events and includes a Steam Rally Section. Bromyard is a vibrant town with a Spring Festival in May and a Folk Festival in September.

Kington

The restored Church of Saint Mary, dating from the 12th century, provides views of the beautiful Arrow Valley. Of the county's towns only Hereford itself and Kington had Medieval castles sited within the town. The site of Kington Castle is hidden in trees near the church. The castle once controlled access and communications along the Medieval road to New Radnor and across the River Arrow at this critical border location. The modern by-pass allows visitors to explore this now peaceful town and Kington, too, has a most enjoyable Festival, which lasts for two weeks in June.

Kington is an ideal base for walking in the Welsh hills. The very popular Offa's Dyke Footpath, opened in 1971, follows the Welsh-English border for about 177 miles. One of the best preserved sections, seen in the photograph facing page 73, is on Rushock Hill, north of the town, while Hergest Ridge is lovely countryside with outstanding views. The Mortimer Trail to Ludlow passes sites connected with the Medieval barons.

Ross-on-Wye and Wilton Castle

This magnificent view of Ross shows the town's position on raised ground above a meander of the River Wye. The restored 13th- / 14th-century Church of Saint Mary overlooks the flood plain. To the right of the river bridge is Wilton Castle, built to control the crossing but burnt in the Civil War. The Market Hall of 1650, now a Heritage Centre, can be seen at the triple road-junction in the centre of Ross. Until recently the Ross International Festival was held in August.

Gloucester to Hereford Canal

The Gloucester, Ledbury to Hereford Canal was started with a 1791 Act of Parliament designed to cut a canal from the River Severn at Gloucester in order to transport coal from the Forest of Dean collieries to Hereford. Its route was via Ledbury, which it almost reached in 1798, with a branch to Newent. However, it did not reach Hereford until 1845, being the last long canal built in Britain. It was commercially efficient for only a very short time, and it was leased to the Great Western and West Midland Railways in 1862, its route becoming a part of the railway line in 1881. The canal was far too late as the railways were already seen as the future for both commerce and passengers.

In the middle distance in this long view west from Monkhide, the tree-lined canal passes under the modern, and once Roman, road west to Hereford. To the right of the canal between the two roads there can be seen the curving traces of Medieval ridge-and-furrow ploughing. Note, too, the orchards that are still a characteristic feature of Herefordshire.

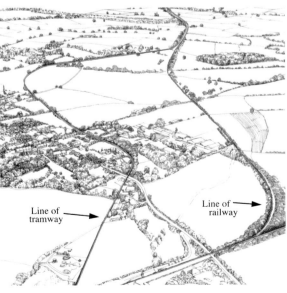

Line of tramway

Line of railway

Eardisley Tramroad and Railway

The tramway from Brecon to Hay, where wagons were pulled by horses, was extended to Eardisley in 1818 and then turned north towards Kington and the limestone quarries at Burlingjobb and Dolyhir near Old Radnor.

The part of the tramroad north from Eardisley, centre left, was acquired by the Kington and Eardisley Railway and much of the railway was laid, starting in 1863, to follow the old tramway. During the Second World War an additional railway line was built just outside Eardisley to service an oil and petrol dump for the U.S.A. army at the military camp at Hergest / Kington (see page 96). The railway became part of the Great Western Railway in 1897 and was finally closed in 1962.

Eardisley was the junction station that connected the Kington and Eardisley Railway with the Hereford, Hay and Brecon Railway which can be seen here as a straight line across the bottom of the photograph.

Great Western Railway at Hatfield / Docklow

Winding into the distance towards the south-east is the disused line of the Leominster to Bromyard section of the former Worcester, Bromyard and Leominster Railway, finally completed in 1897 after the line became part of the Great Western Railway. It still cuts an impressive swathe through the north Herefordshire landscape. The pattern of fields under snow shows clearly where field boundaries have been crossed by the later railway. Although popular with the seasonal hop-pickers, the Leominster to Bromyard section eventually became uneconomic and was closed in 1952.

Fencote Abbey Farm, in a detached portion of the Parish of Docklow, in the foreground to the right of the railway, was a part of the lands of Leominster nunnery. According to Domesday the abbess held it before 1066 and still held it in 1086. This suggests she was allowed to retire here, perhaps in compensation when the nunnery was dissolved in 1046. Was she the Eadgifu mentioned on page 43? Domesday shows that the Normans also left her in residence although little is known about the site. However, the field left of the farm, *284 Fish Pool Meadow* and above it *304 The Bank* have shadow marks of a bank and ditch crossing them. Further shadow marks of the square corner of a bank can also be seen centre. None are field boundaries so perhaps they are remnants of the abbess' home.

Sand-and-gravel extraction at Wellington, in the Lugg Valley

Sand-and-gravel extraction has been vastly extended in recent years. Here the grades are being sorted. In 1986 excavation ahead of gravel extraction by Redland Aggregates at Marden Quarry, Wellington, led to the discoveries of a prehistoric enclosure and a small Roman villa. The possible extension of gravel extraction along the Lugg Valley is controversial as it threatens archaeological sites and would disturb the unique lammas meadows near Lugwardine, common meadows where grazing is allowed from 1 August, Lammas, to 2 February, Candlemas.

Stone quarry at Gatley Park

The Gatley Park quarry at Aymestrey is shielded from the rest of the estate, belonging to the Dunne family, by James' Fall, an area of ancient woodland seen on the right. The quarrying is for limestone for the building industry and for roads. The patterns of modern extractive industries, if less than beautiful at ground level, make spectacular photographs from the air.

Industrial estate and by-pass at Leominster

The commercial pattern of many towns, in Herefordshire as elsewhere, has been radically changed in recent years by the building of by-passes and the construction of industrial estates and supermarkets, often far away from the original centres of the towns. Here at Leominster the by-pass, opened on 1 November 1988 around the eastern side of the town, is located alongside the railway, originally the Shrewsbury and Hereford Railway, running north from Hereford. In the centre foreground the modern buildings of the Southern Avenue Industrial Estate contrast sharply in scale and character with the older parts of Leominster beyond.

Leominster still retains the ground-plan of narrow, attractive, Medieval streets with timber-framed buildings, the most notable of which is Grange Court, built in 1633 by John Abel as a Town Hall and originally sited in Broad Street. It is now near the Priory Church which remains a focal point for the town. Leominster is a thriving town, the second largest after Hereford, and Corn Square is the venue for the weekly market. Its wealth and reputation in the Medieval period were based on the trade in fleeces, the wool being known locally as 'Leominster Ore'. Now it is known for its antique shops and Fine Art sales rooms.

Wyevale Nurseries, Hereford

There has been a horticultural nursery at King's Acre since the 18th century and, in the 19th century John Cranston, the son of the then owner, founded the Hereford and West of England Rose Society. Trading as King's Acre Nursery, the enterprise specialised in fruit trees, introducing the new varieties of King's Acre Berry, King's Acre Pippin and King's Acre Bountiful. Bought by H. Williamson in 1931, the company is now Wyevale Nurseries, with branches all over the country. The straight line running through the nursery from upper left towards lower right 'fossilises' the former line of the Midland Railway.

A factory in the rural landscape (above)
The Cadbury, Trebor, Bassett Factory at Marlbrook / Fordsbridge was built in 1937 on fields that were once orchards. It is a collecting point for local milk used in chocolate production at the main Cadbury factory at Bourneville. The ponds are part of the effluent treatment plant. The Leominster by-pass joins the curving line of the older Leominster to Hereford road just beyond the photograph to the right, before the steep climb over Dinmore Hill (see page 15).

Military Camp at Kington

The military camp shown above, south of Kington in the valley of the River Arrow, was variously known as Hergest Camp, Huntington Park Camp or Kington Camp. The land was requisitioned in 1940 and the 5th Gloucesters, 2nd Warwickshires and 8th Worcesters were stationed here after the evacuation from Dunkirk. In 1941 reconstruction was started by Wimpeys U.K. for the U.S. 693rd Field Artillery Unit who were stationed here in 1943-1944 to wait for the D-Day landings. Visitors to the camp included the British Prime Minister, Winston Churchill, and the American General George S. Patton Junior, nick-named 'Blood-and-Guts'. The photograph shows some huts still in use, while others in the foreground have decayed leaving only earthwork platforms to show where they once stood.

Army huts, Moreton-on-Lugg

The military camp at Moreton-on-Lugg, used by the U.S. Army during the Second World War, was manned by a bomb disposal unit until quite recently. Here the 'nissen' huts, in varying stages of use or decay, form a bold and attractive pattern that can only be seen from the air, the huts otherwise lying hidden behind an impenetrable screen of trees. By the time this book is published they will all have been removed.

Rotherwas Munitions Compound, Hereford

Rotherwas was a large estate belonging to the Bodenham family whose house was destroyed by fire in 1907, being finally demolished in 1925, leaving only the chapel and the remains of the walled kitchen garden. The estate became the site of a Royal Ordnance Factory in 1916, at its peak in 1918 employing 5,943 people, more than two-thirds of them women.

This photograph, taken shortly after the vegetation had been cut back in 1998, shows the 30-acre North Section of the site. The oldest feature is the huge rectangular foundation of a building, lower left, one of a pair built in 1916. Here shell cases were received by train, run along overhead rails within the building, cleaned, de-greased and painted. While the companion building still stands complete with rails, and in one place shows the circular marks of heavy shell cases on the concrete floor, this site is shown in the photograph being used for composting green waste.

The 'oval' concrete blast walls, centre, built 1919-1938, each had four entrances. In the centre of each 'oval' was a timber hut with an asbestos roof, whose concrete foundation survives. Each housed ten to twelve girls who put fuses in the shells. The entrances at each end, supplemented by two gaps in the long lengths of the blast walls, were to allow the possibility of escape by the workers in the event of an explosion. The straight lines between the blast wall 'oval' groups are well-made raised concrete and asphalt roads.

Other buildings between the 'ovals' are air-raid shelters, equipped with seating, chemical toilets screened by felt curtains and window blocks to forestall a gas attack. The three long seats provided were concrete topped by wooden laths overlain with hardboard to give a degree of comfort.

The long building in the field top right was the Picric Acid Bond Store, kept locked, and placed away from other buildings with a large safety area around it. Picric acid, or trinitrophenol, was used from 1771 as a yellow synthetic dye until in the 1880s its explosive properties were realised. The circular filter beds of the later sewage plant are on the extreme right. Other areas of the 250-acre estate are now an industrial park, but access to the area depicted is restricted.

Pembridge: a typical Herefordshire village

Pembridge is known as one of Herefordshire's most attractive 'black-and-white' villages, with many timber buildings surviving from the 15th through to the 18th century. It has become a popular place for people to live, although, as with all the villages, expansion is limited to prevent them losing their distinctive village character.

Top photograph: Here Pembridge shows how villages expand along the roads and field-by-field often from the central focus of the church, market square and original main road.

Lower photograph: The 13th- / 14th-century Church of Saint Mary has an unusual detached Medieval bell tower, one of only seven in the county. It has enormous posts, four of which are early 13th century, and 15th- / 16th-century stone walls. The narrow loop-holes in the walls suggest that it was a place of refuge and holes still to be seen in the door are thought to be from gunshot. The timber-framed market hall, with 17th-century posts and mouldings, and the early 17th-century New Inn occupy a typically triangular 'island' at the junction of the three roads on the right. This was the market place of the Medieval borough. The market hall posts have notches which were probably to hold planks used as stalls, while two stones on the east side are thought to be 'nails' where transactions were agreed, giving rise to the saying of 'paying on the nail'.

Weobley and its motte-and-bailey castle

Top photograph: This shows the picturesque main street of Weobley, with the Church of Saint Peter and Saint Paul just out of shot at bottom left and the castle beyond this view to the top right. The triangular area of grass marks the wider area of the road once used as a market place. The aerial view-point clearly shows the way that the modern bound-aries between the houses still reflect the narrow burgage plots of the planned Medieval town, though some properties now occupy more than one plot.

Lower photograph: The motte-and-bailey castle at the top of the photograph originally belonged to the de Lacy family. It was captured by King Stephen in 1138. Most unusually, there is a plan drawn by Silas Taylor of the castle in 1655, which shows that it had developed by then as a rectangular stone castle with six towers on the curtain wall, four towers on the rectangular keep on the original motte, and two houses in the bailey. This photograph does suggest straight outer walls, though more curving than Taylor depicted. The earthworks as they survive today more closely reflect the typical curving line of the motte-and-bailey castle in its original form.

Bulmers Cider Factory in Hereford

Bulmers cider vats and factory off Plough Lane are sited alongside housing and open fields. Cider was recommended for good health and used on ships in the 18th century to counter scurvy. There were various strengths, the first press being the strongest, and the second press, after further water was added, producing 'small cider' used as labourers' wages. They were entitled to extra at harvest time — up to 24 pints a day! By the 19th century there was large-scale production with several hundred cider-making firms in the county, one of which was H.P. Bulmer Ltd., now part of Scottish Courage, the U.K. beer division of the Scottish & Newcastle Group. Bulmers started production in 1888 and, despite losing its independent status, is still the largest cider producer in the world. Westons' Cider has been established at Much Marcle since 1880, and another producer is Dunkertons Cider Company at Pembridge. Probably the best apple for an unblended cider is still the 'Kingston Black', having the best natural balance of tannin to acid. In 1993 the Three Counties Cider and Perry Association was formed to focus expertise and promote the industry.

'Blue' Trees

Nets, here coloured blue, are a convenient way to protect and catch fruit, especially cherries, preventing bruising and the depredations of birds. Orchards are still common in Herefordshire, though in many the standard trees have been replaced by bush trees.

Ancient and modern at Monnington Straddle

At Monnington Straddle, near Vowchurch, the Norman motte in the trees lies alongside a modern farm, now equipped with the new barns which are such a common feature in present-day Herefordshire. This is also the site of the manor house, which was once the home of Margaret, one of Owain Glyndwr's daughters. Glyndwr himself is thought to be buried nearby. Such a farm still cultivates the same fields that have been the basis of agriculture for centuries. The field size and the techniques used may have changed but cattle and sheep are still farmed alongside cereals and other crops. Mixed farming remains important in Herefordshire.

There is much in Herefordshire that would be recognisable to those who lived in the past. The topography, rivers, soil quality and potential productivity have changed little, and the road system may even include tracks first used in prehistoric times. While there has been destruction, there has also been continuity, but the most noticeable changes are in the people. We are healthier now, eat varied food, are better housed and educated. Agriculture is still important but there are increased work opportunities and each town has its industrial park. In 1974 Herefordshire lost its county status when it was joined to Worcestershire. The amalgamation was not viewed as a success and in 1999 Herefordshire became an independent county once again. Herefordians have survived through wars, poverty and prosperity for centuries, believing that Herefordshire is a special and beautiful place. We hope that this book has given a glimpse of all it has to offer.

Further Reading

Invaluable sources of information for Herefordshire are: The *Transactions* of the Woolhope Naturalists' Field Club, where the various papers by individual authors are most useful, the collections in Herefordshire Record Office, which also include copies of all; The Herefordshire Field-Name Survey booklets covering every parish, and The Sites and Monuments Record for Herefordshire, at Herefordshire Archaeology and also now available online at www.smr.herefordshire.gov.uk. For further information on aerial photography see Chris. Musson, *Wales from the Air*, Royal Commission on the Ancient and Historical Monuments of Wales. For information about field-names see *Transactions* Volume XLVIII 1996 part III and Ruth E. Richardson, Herefordshire Field-Names, in D. Whitehead and J. Eisel, editors, *A Herefordshire Miscellany*, 2000 Lapridge Publications.

Numerous books and articles have been consulted for particular chapters. Books on local people, families and the countryside, can be found in the Local History sections of Libraries. These include excellent histories of the towns. Books on the county as a whole include:

G. Children and G. Nash, *Prehistoric Sites of Herefordshire*, 1994, Logaston Press.

E. Heath-Agnew, *A History of Hereford Cattle and their Breeders*, 1983, Duckworth.

N. Pevsner, *The Buildings of England, Herefordshire*, 1963, Penguin.

R.E. Richardson, 'The Potential Farmland of the Iron Age and Romano-British Periods' in the Herefordshire Area, 1989, unpublished M.Phil. thesis, copy in Herefordshire Record Office.

S.C. Stanford, *The Archaeology of the Welsh Marches*, 1991 revised edition by author.

J.W. Tonkin, *Herefordshire*, 1977, Batsford.

T. Rowley, *The Landscape of the Welsh Marches*, 1986, Michael Joseph, London.

J. and M. West, *A History of Herefordshire*, 1985, Phillimore.

P. White, *The Arrow Valley*, Herefordshire, 2003, Herefordshire Studies in Archaeology Series 2.

D. Whitehead, *A Survey of the Historic Parks & Gardens in Herefordshire*, 2001, Hereford & Worcester Gardens Trust.

Woolhope Naturalists' Field Club, *Herefordshire, its natural history, archaeology and history*, 1954, republished 1971, S.R. Publishers Ltd.

Photo References

Front:	00-MC01-05	21T	00-C-0759	44	99-C-0732	64	02-MB-0030	87	00-C-0536
Rear:	95-MC03	21B	96-C-1366	45	03-CN-0601	66	00-C-0780	88	99-C-0546
Page		22	00-MB-0008	46	95-MB-0923	67	00-C-0123	89	99-C-0250
Title	99-C-0082*	24	99-C-0857	47	99-C-0326*	68T	00-C-0411*	90	00-C-0588
Contents	00-MB-0688	25T	95-C-2079	48T	99-C-0446	68B	99-C-0487	91	00-MB-0593
Foreword	CRM	25B	00-MB-0364	48B	00-C-0560	69T	99-C-0493*	92	00-C-0889
Opposite 1	94-MC02-49	26	00-C-0349	49	01-C-2026	69B	99-C-0513	93T	99-C-0361*
3	99-C-0194	27	99-C-0565*	50	89-MB-028	70T	00-C-0054	93B	99-C-0281*
4T	00-C-0197	28T	96-C-1437	52	99-C-0070	70B	01-C-2008	94	99-C-0324
4B	96-C-1322	28B	CRM	53T	99-C-0469*	71	99-C-0480	95T	00-C-0276
5T	94-C-1058	29	94-C-1168	53B	99-C-0073	72	02-C-0040	95B	99-C-0382
5B	95-C-2139*	30T	97-MC07-10	54T	99-MB-0045	73	00-MB-0820	96T	99-C-0012
6	00-C-0802	30B	90-C-377	54B	99-C-0096	74	00-C-0881	96B	99-C-0364
7	99-C-0186	31	96-C-1421	55	00-C-0247	75	00-C-0030	97	98-C-0041
8	99-MB-0760	32	00-MB-0856	56	99-C-0042	76	95-MB-0892	98T	99-C-0428
12	99-C-0045*	34	94-C-1115	57	99-MB-0081	79	00-C-0522	98B	99-C-0427
13	00-C-0835	35	03-C-1024	58	99-C-0535	80	95-MC03-10	99T	99-C-0433
14	99-C-0098	36	89-C-212	59B	00-MB-0459	81T	00-C-0068	99B	02-MB-0008
15T	96-C-1418	37	95-C-2128	60	00-C-0508	81B	00-C-0384	100T	00-C-0093
15B	99-C-0724	38	95-C-2340	61T	99-C-0444*	82T	00-C-0503	100B	CRM
16	99-C-0520	39	94-MB-0159	61B	00-C-0525	82B	99-C-0497	101	99-C-0471*
19	99-C-0522	40	94-C-1157	62T	99-C-0374	83	99-C-0459		
20T	99-C-0055	41	90-C-230	62B	00-C-0567	84	95-MB-0898		
20B	00-C-0738	42	00-MC01-08	63	99-C-0352	86	00-C-0648		